Usborne

Decorations

to cut, fold & stick

Illustrated by Amy Blay

Designed by Hannah Ahmed

Steps written by Fiona Watt and illustrated by Chris Arrowsmith and Non Figg

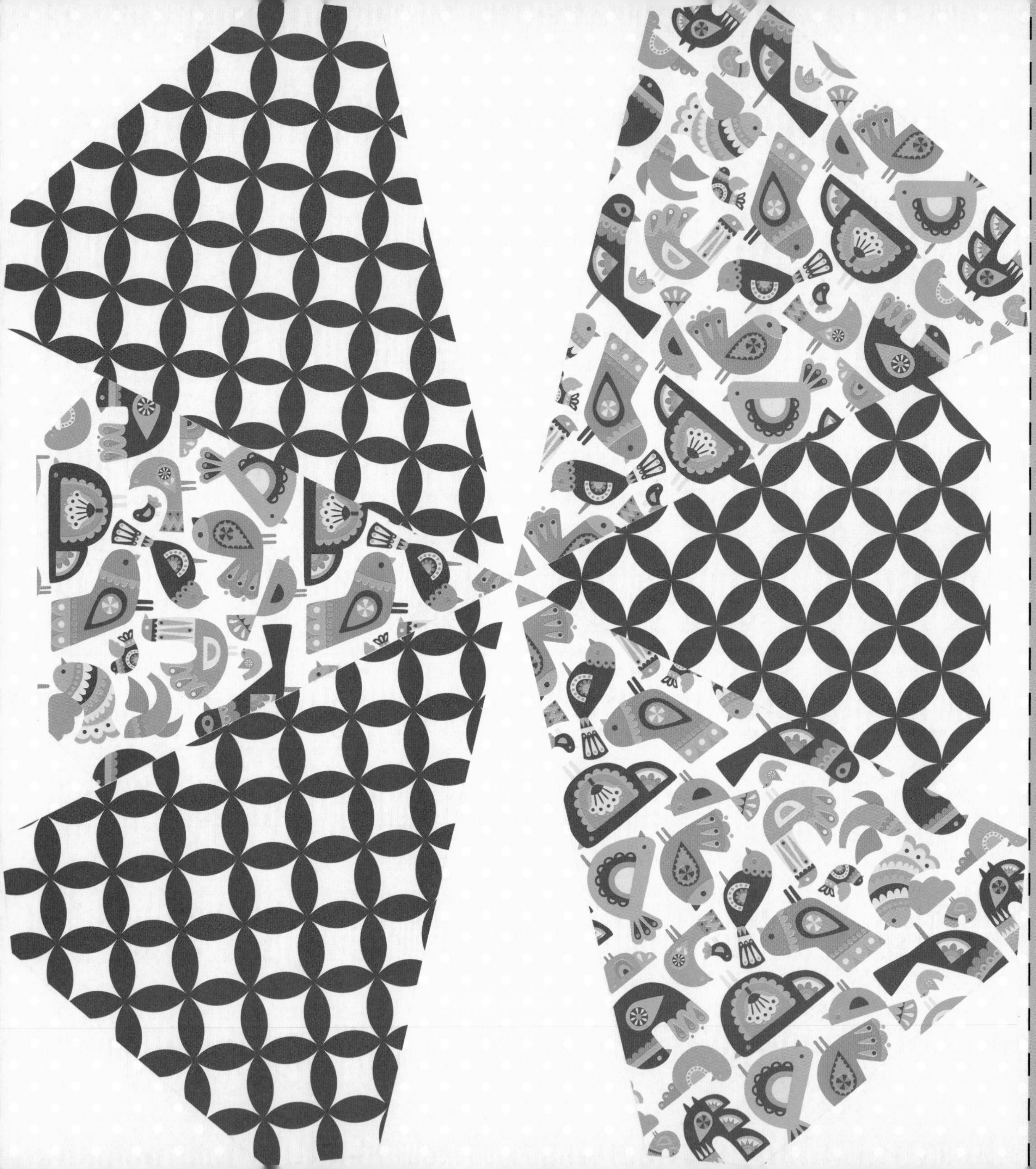

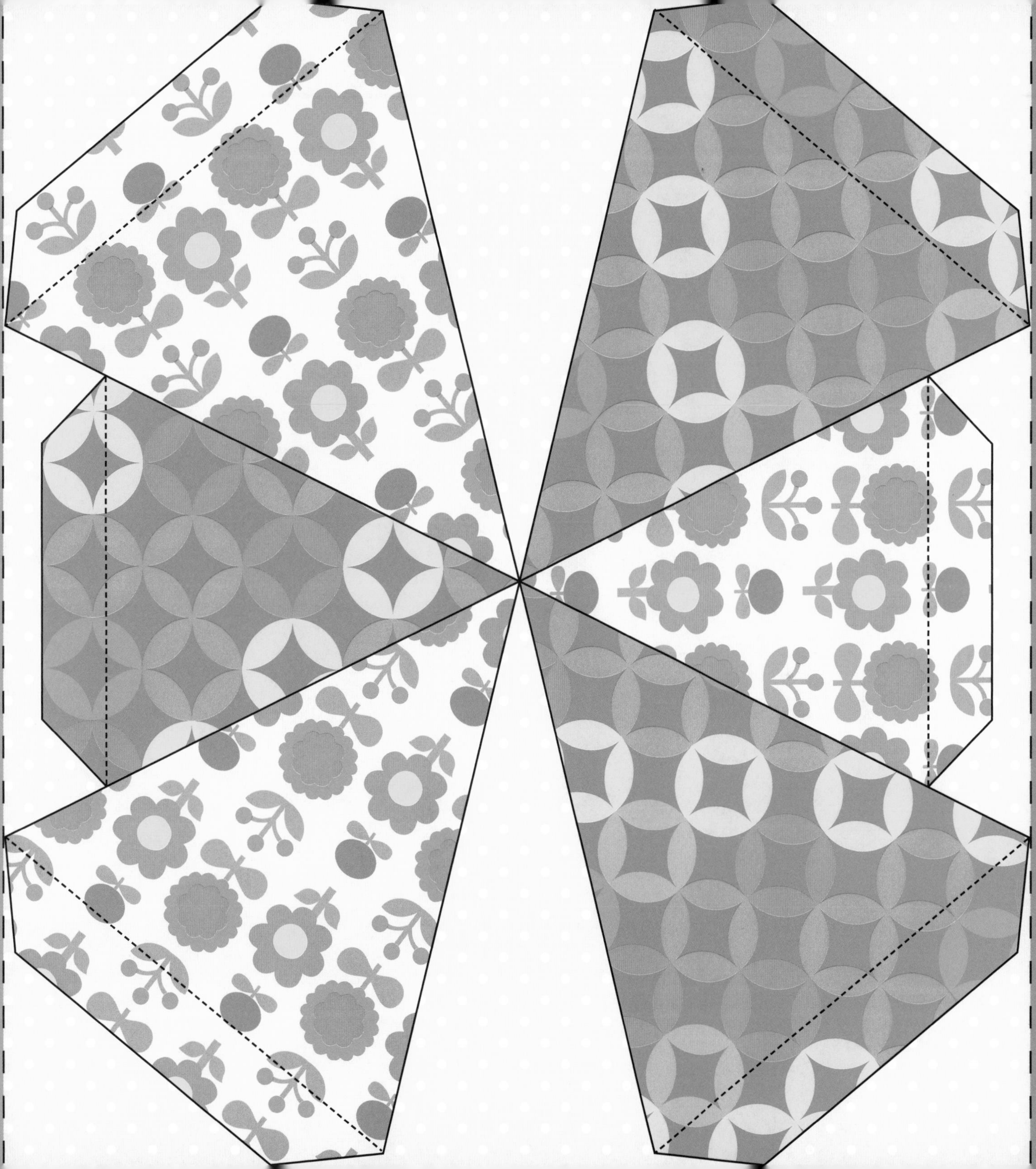

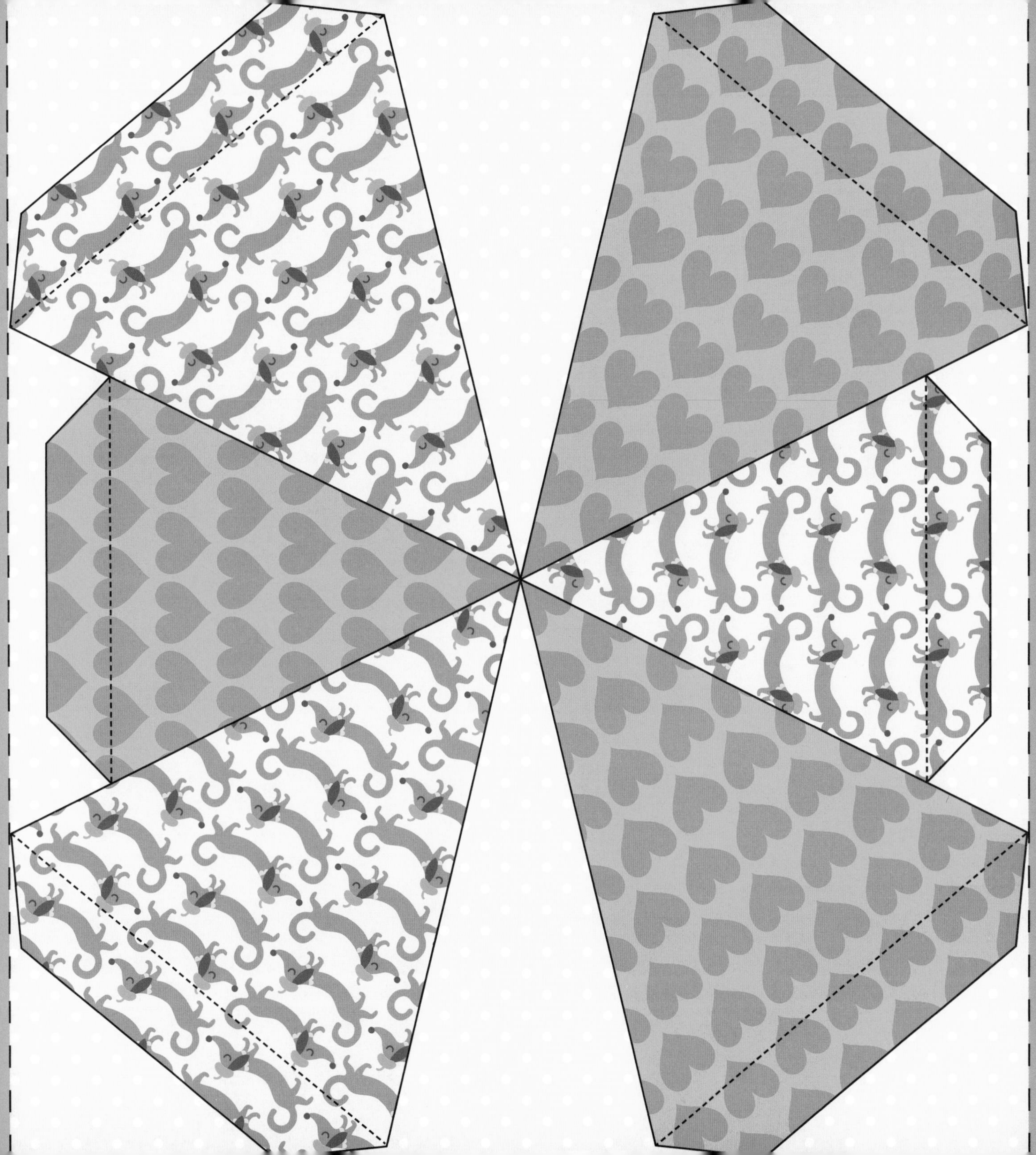

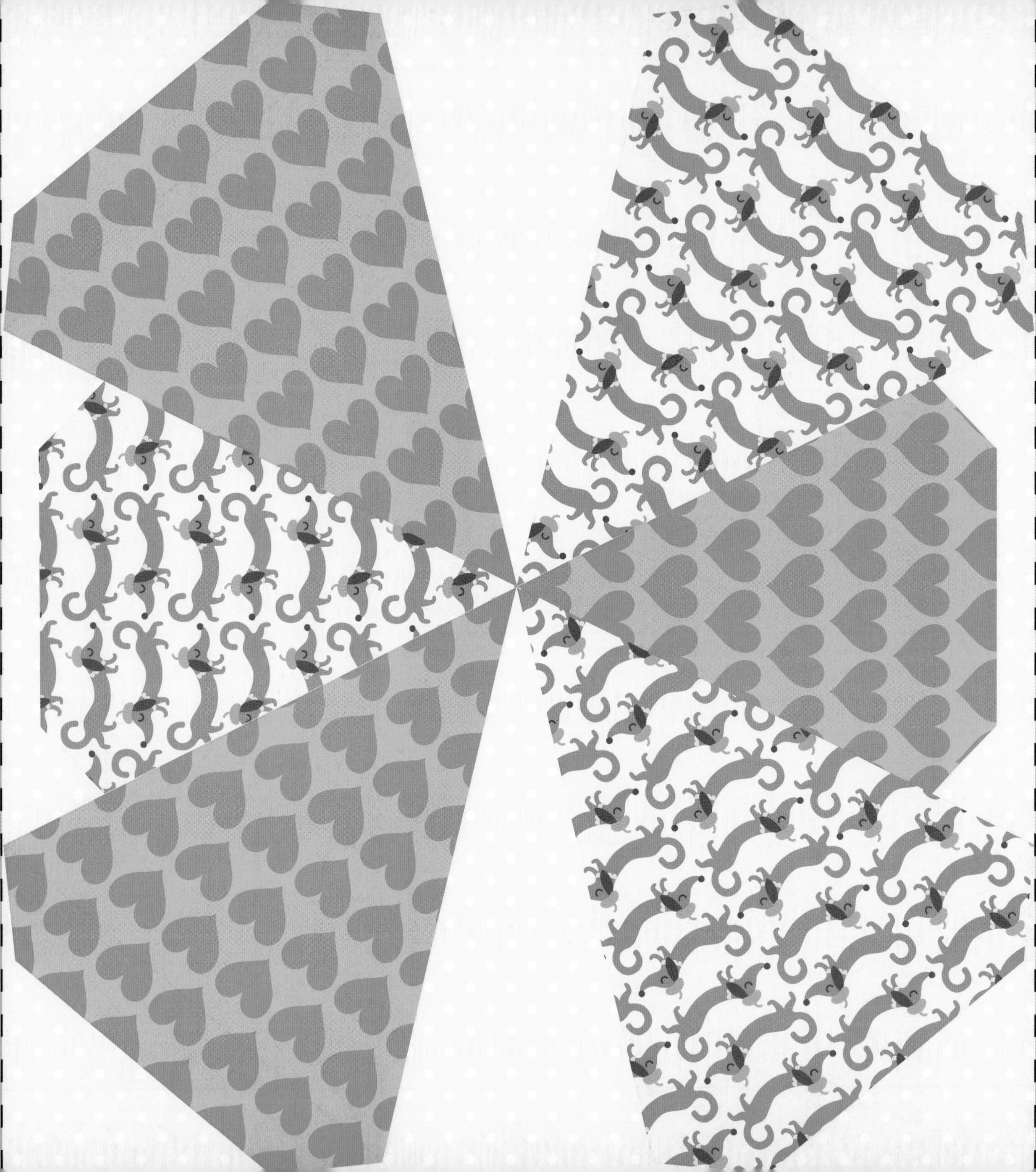

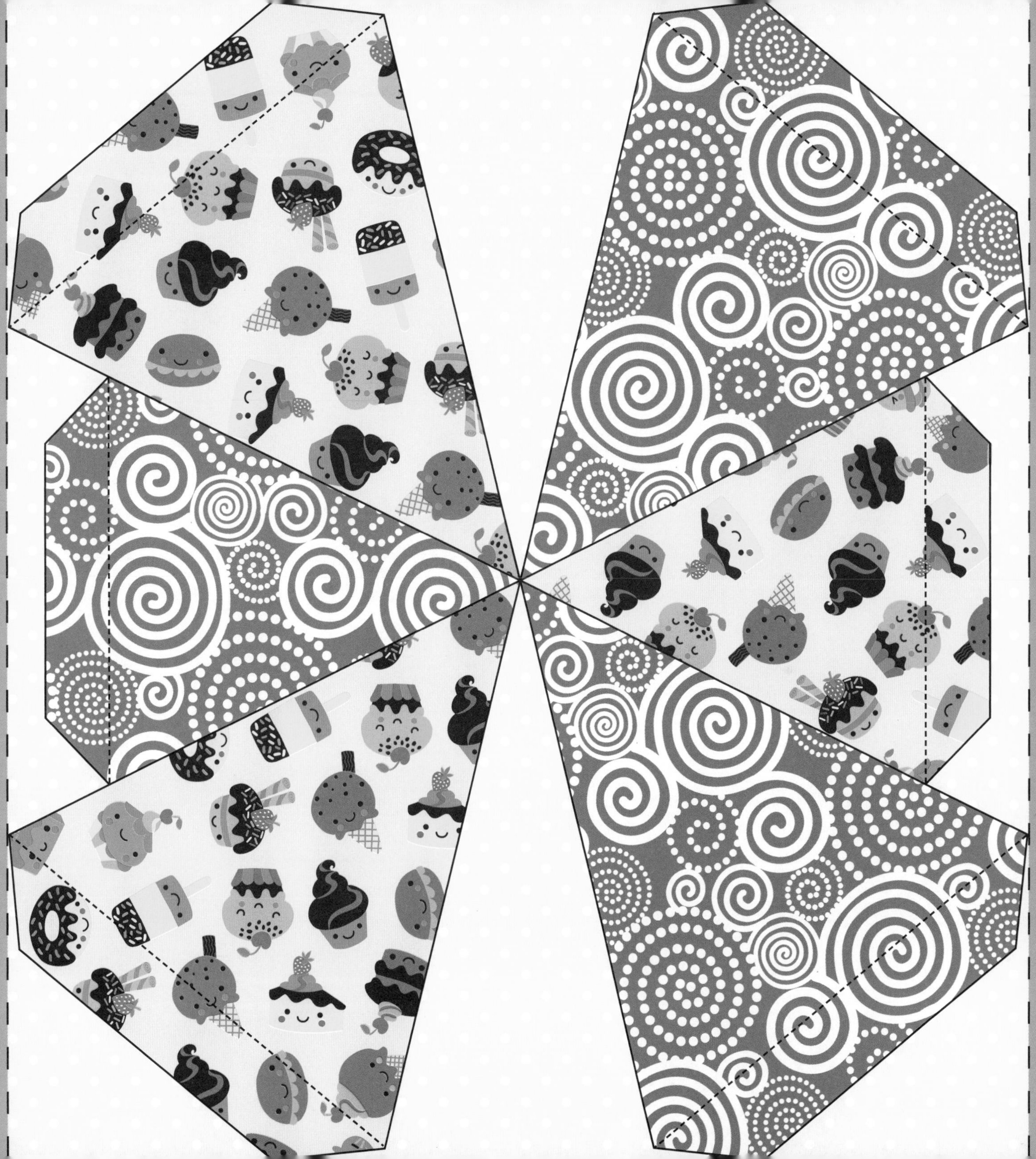

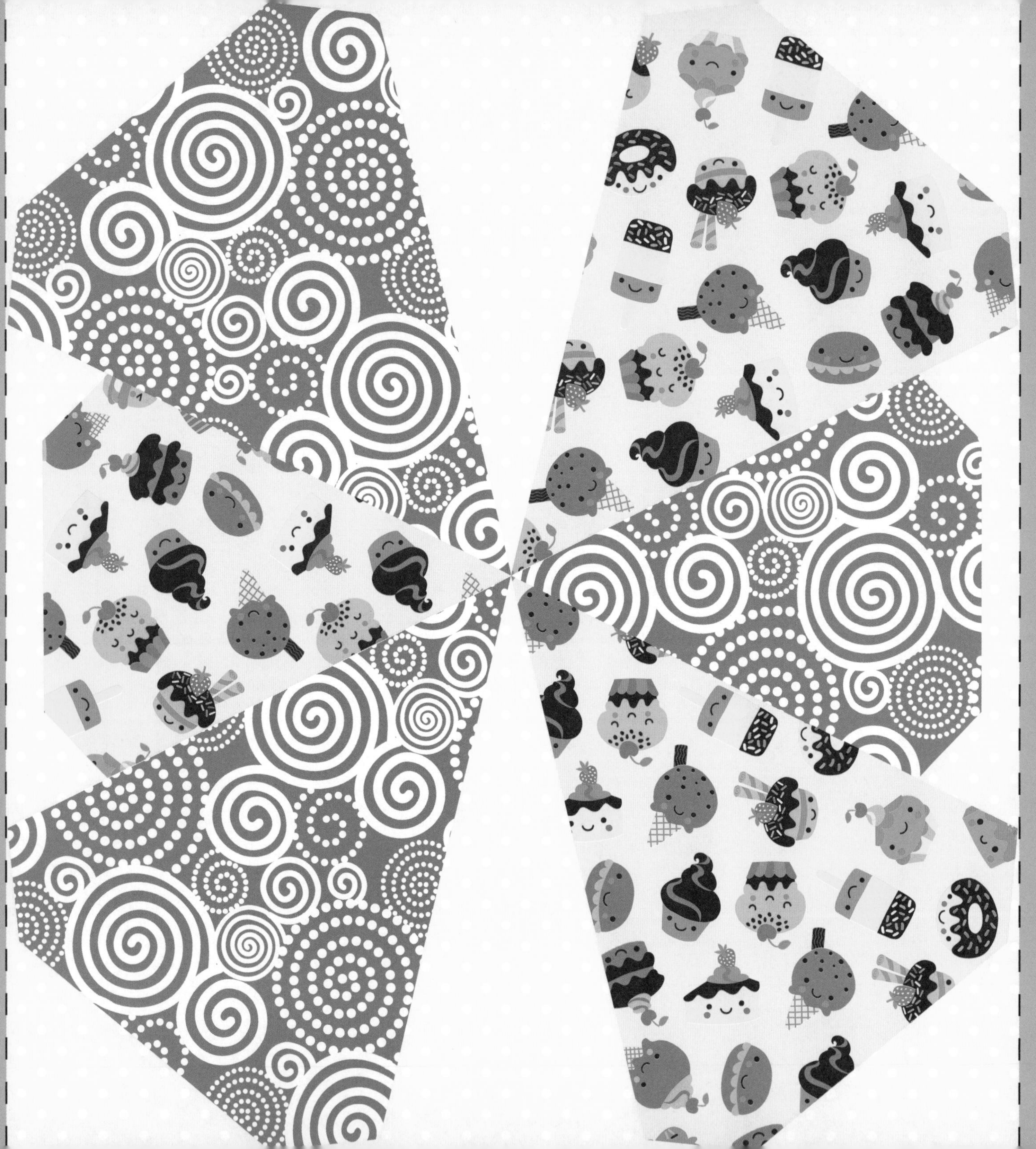

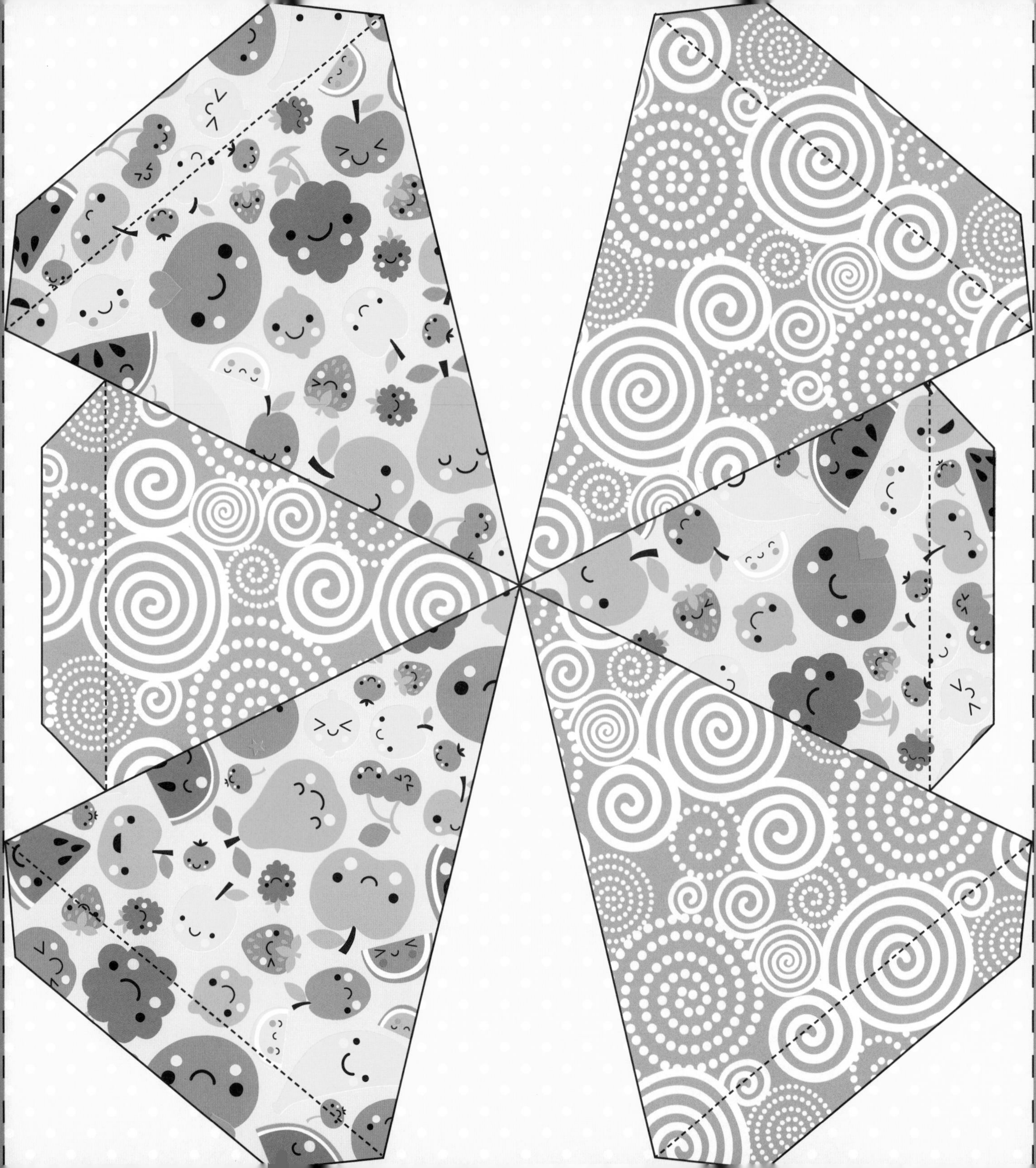

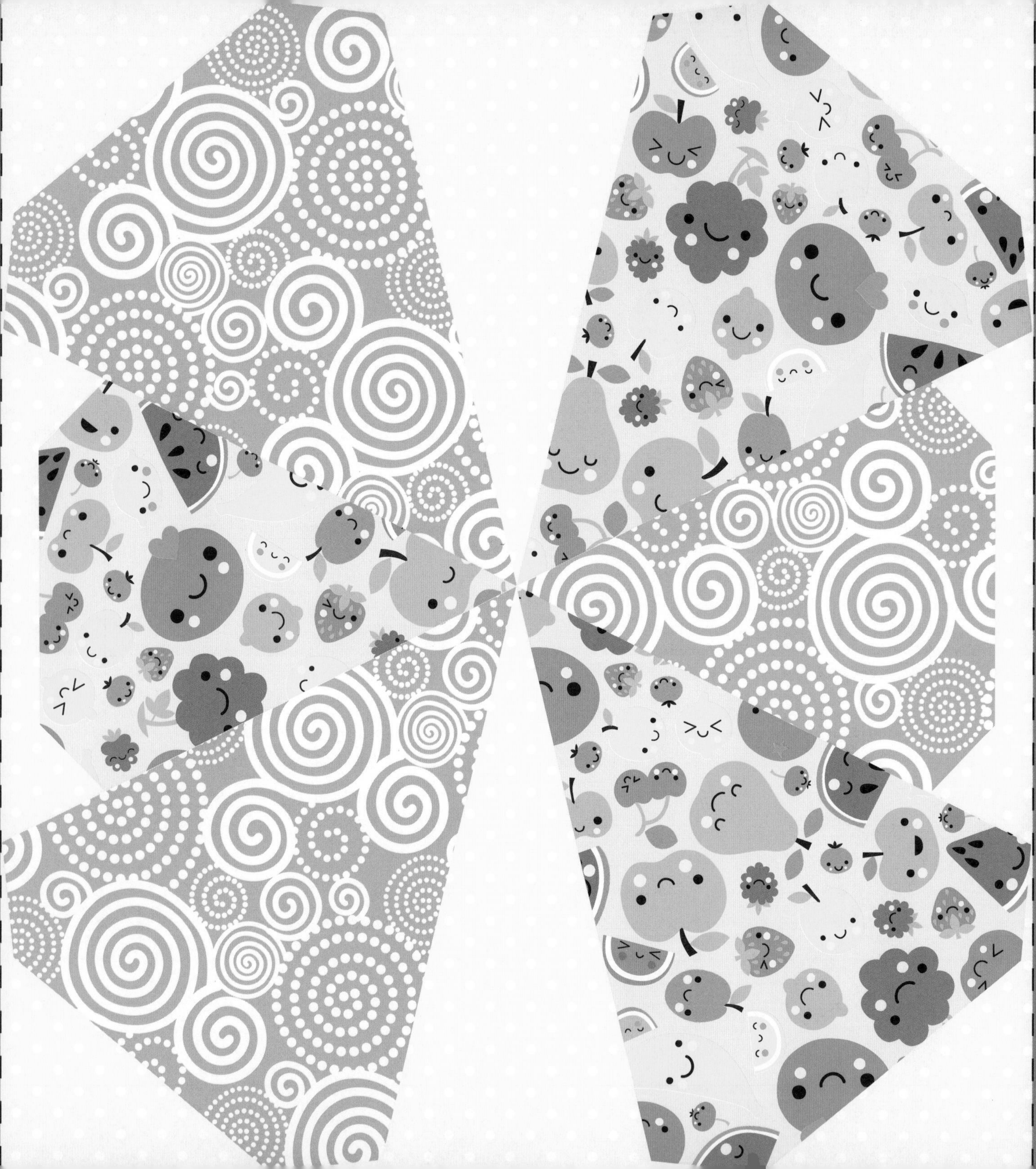

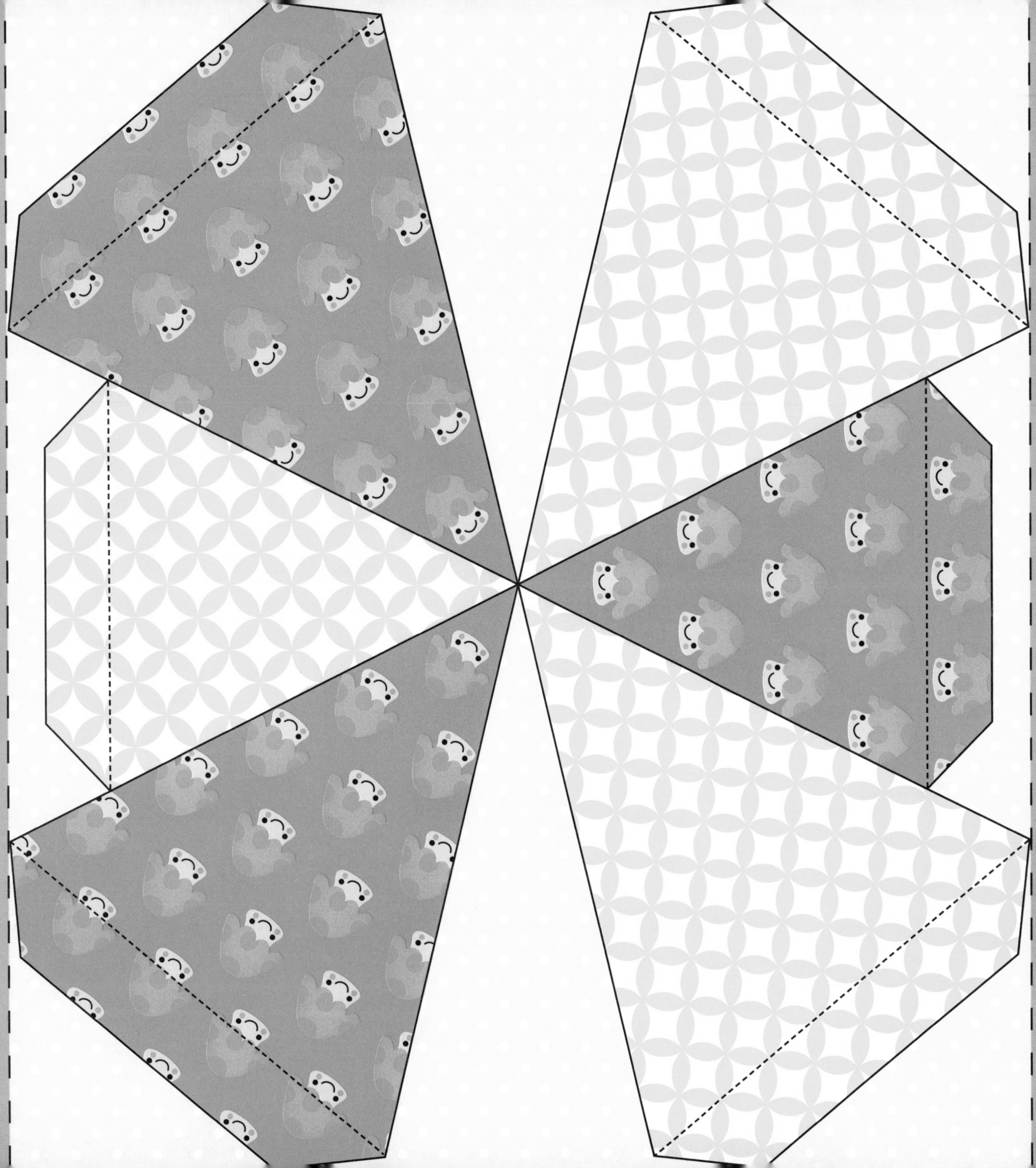

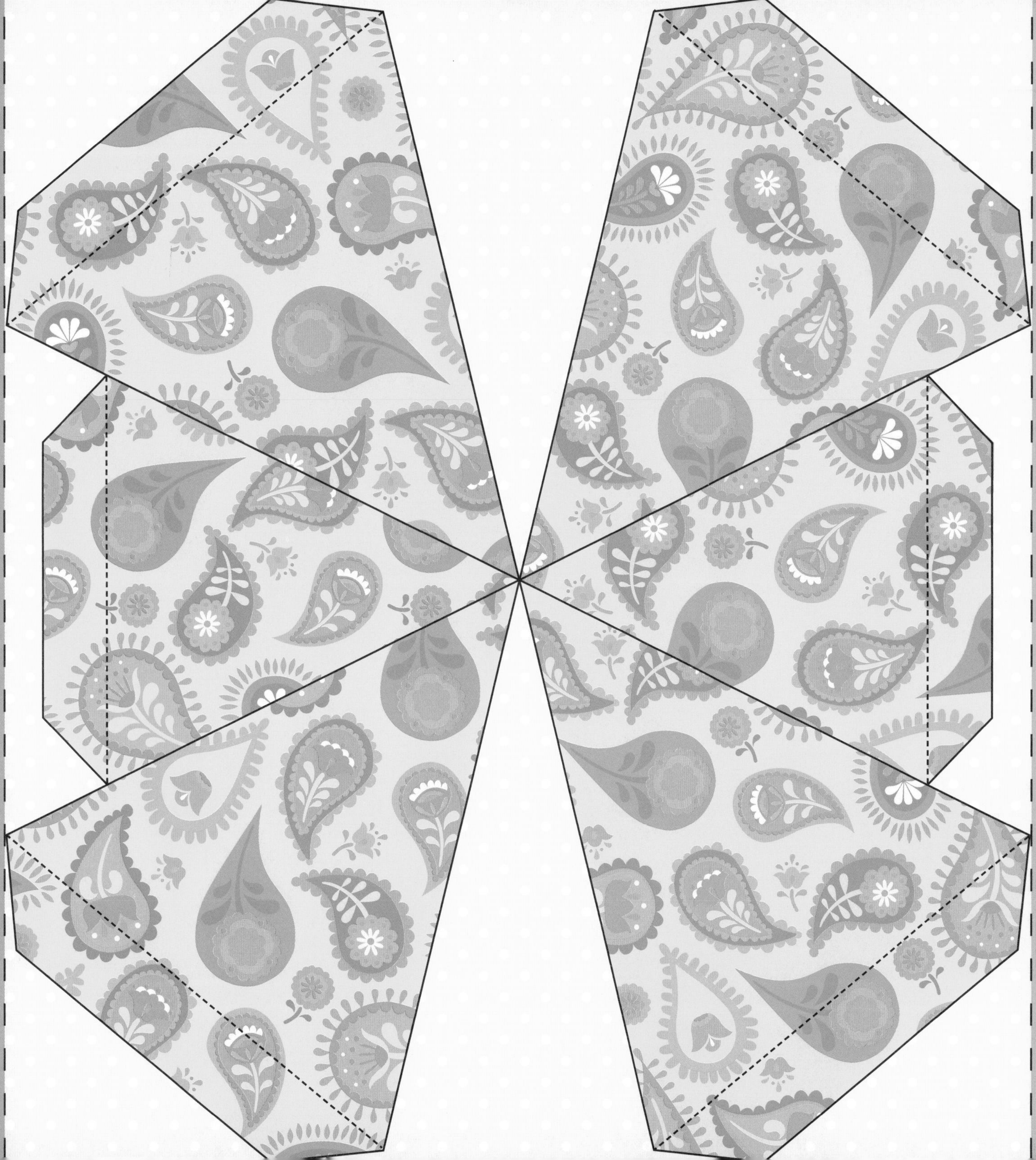

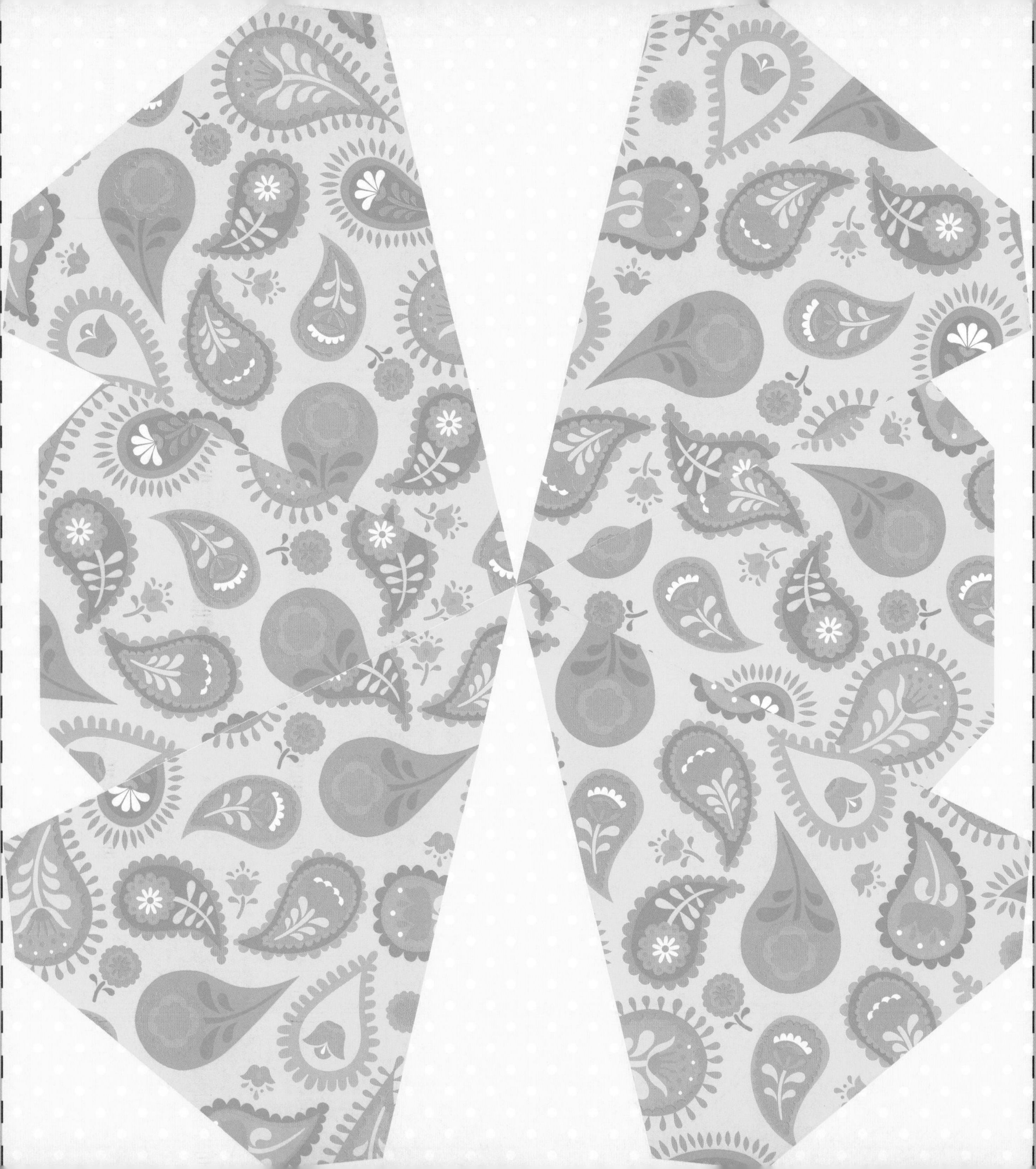

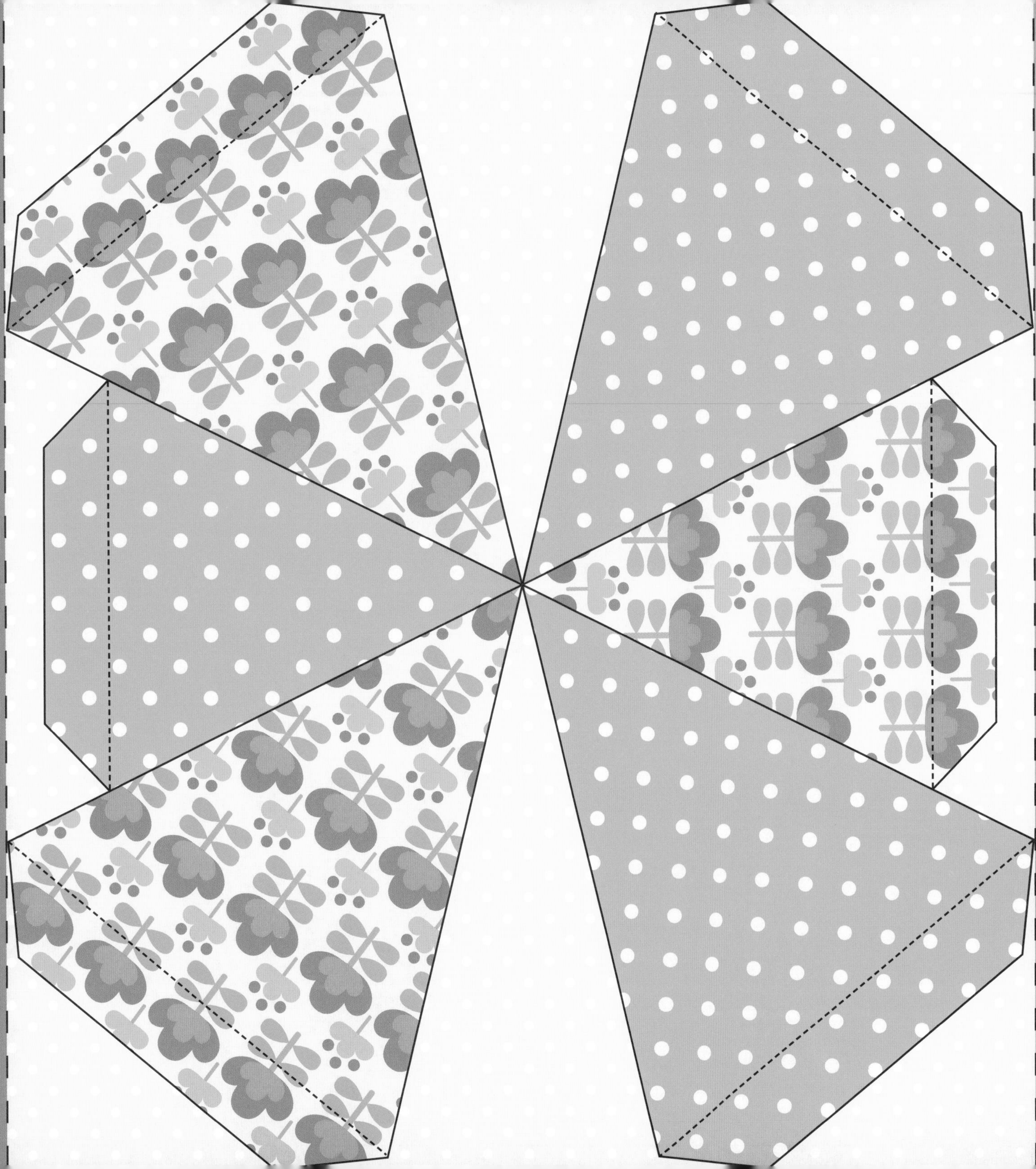

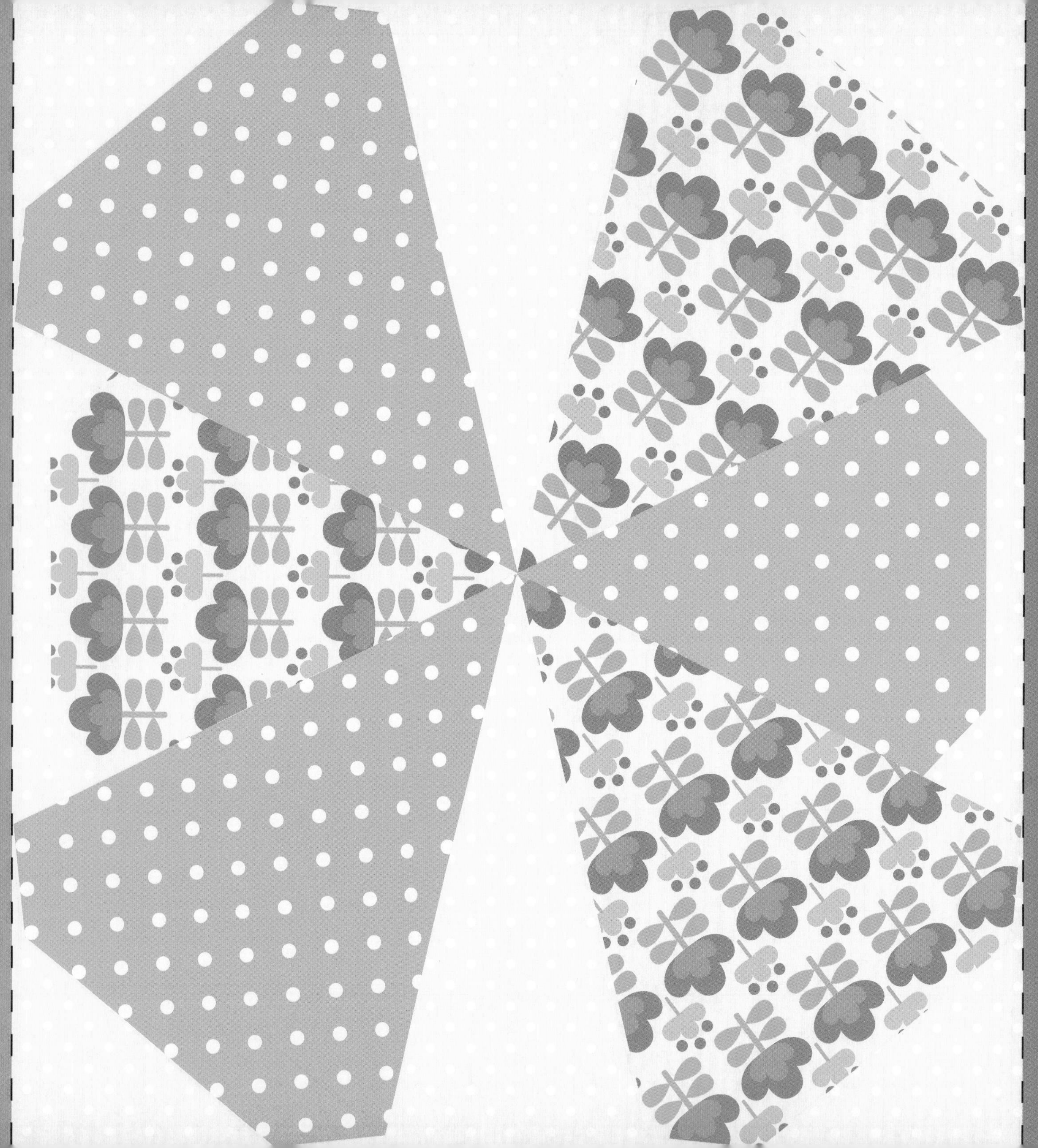

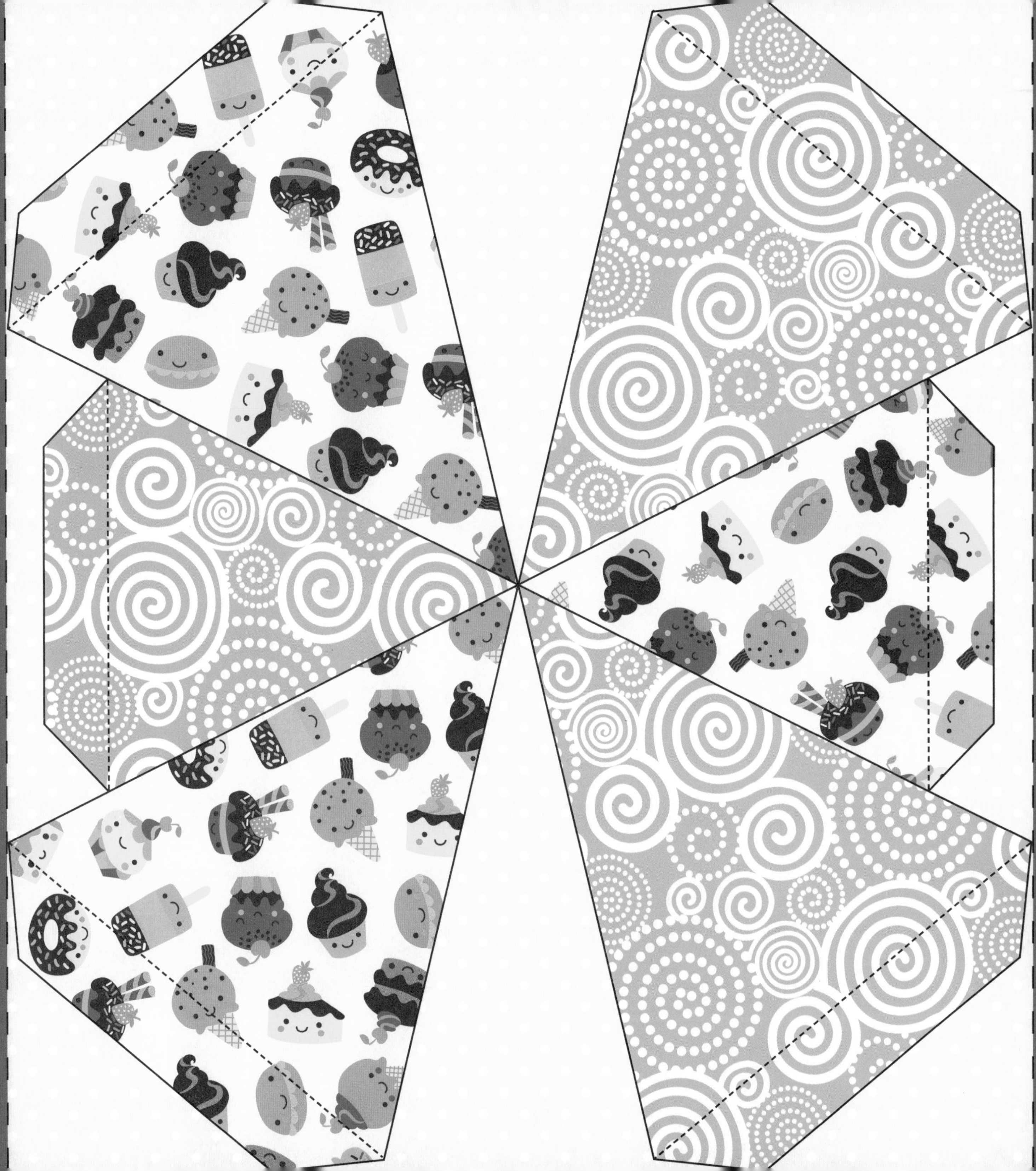

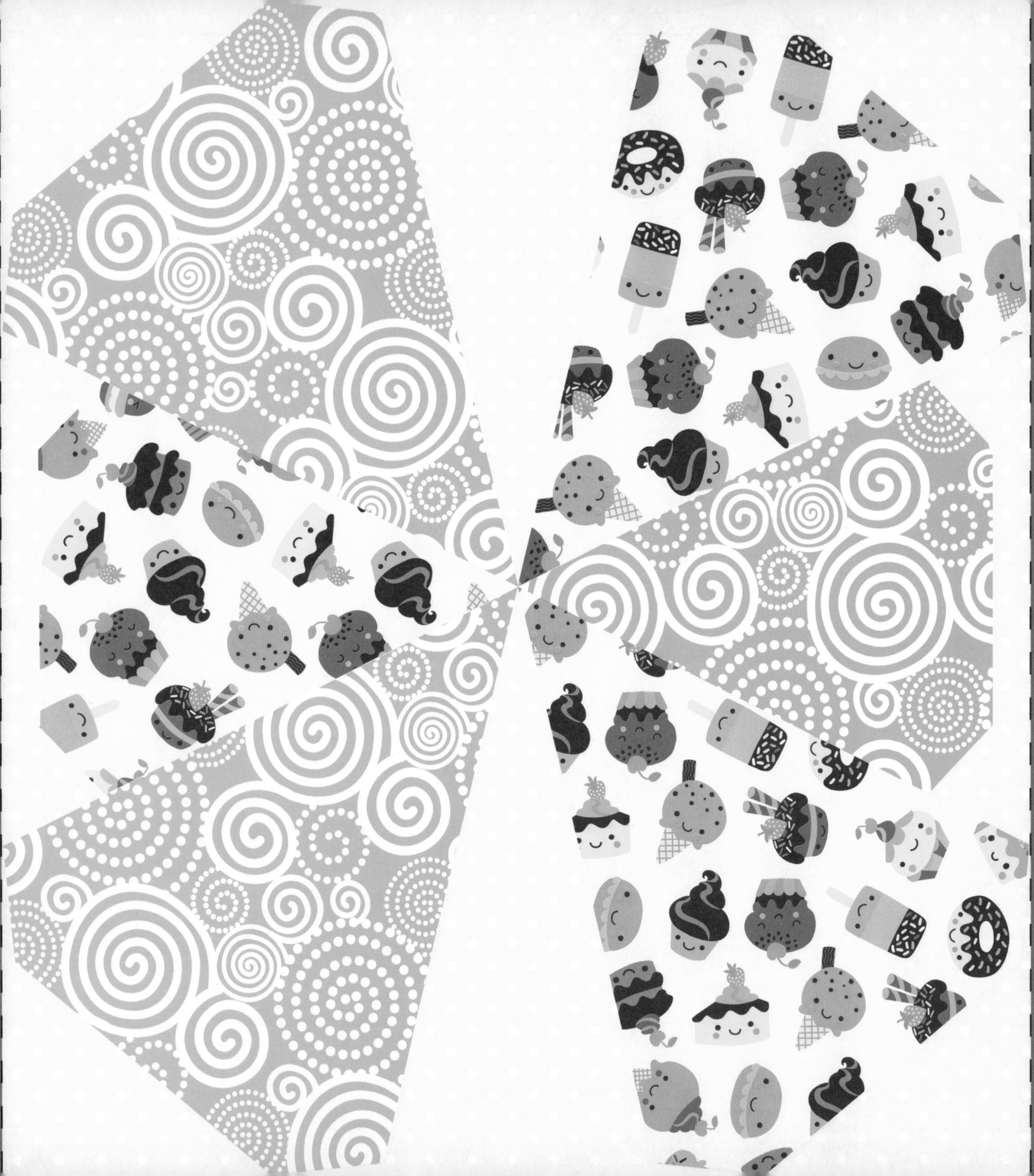

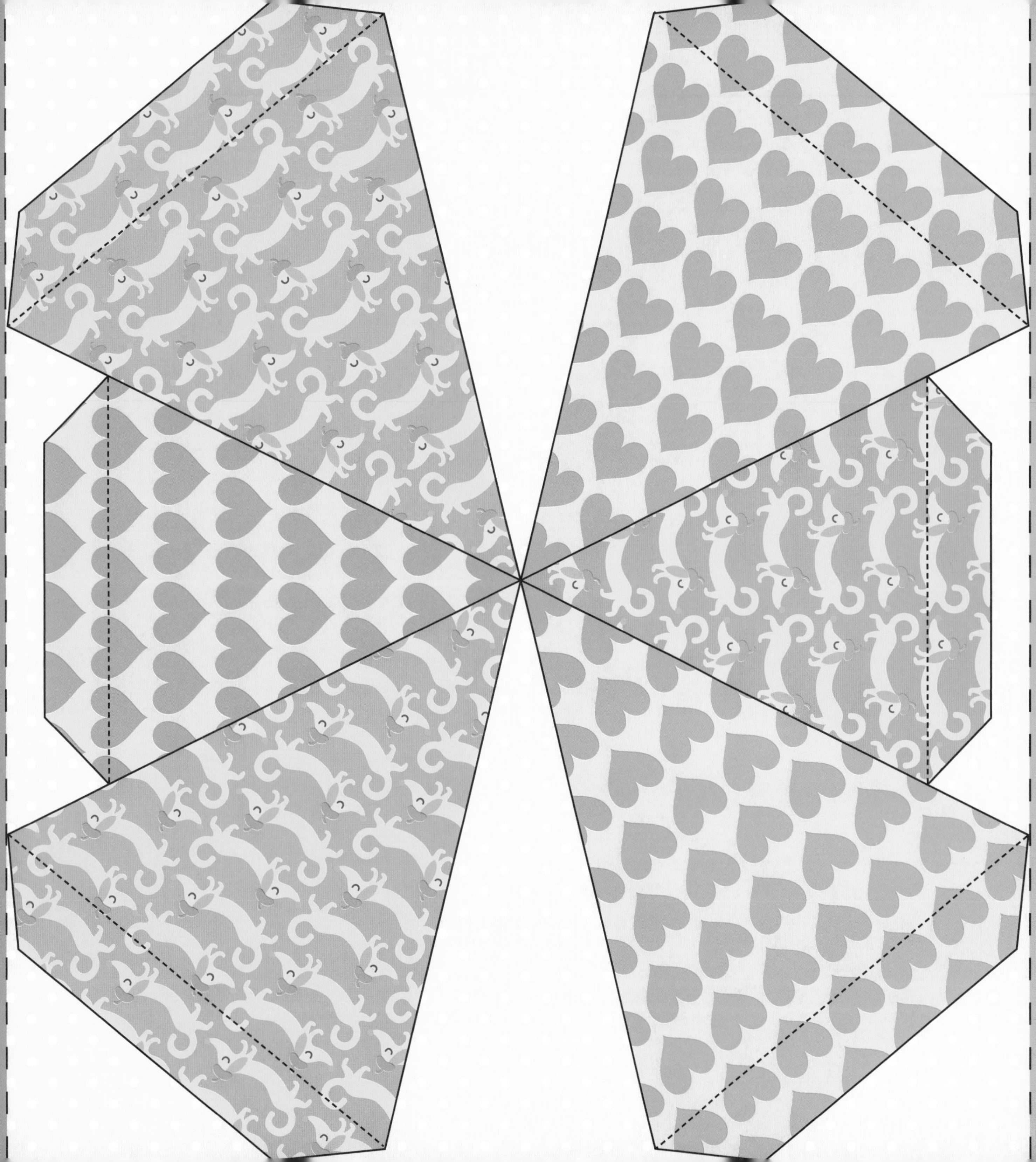

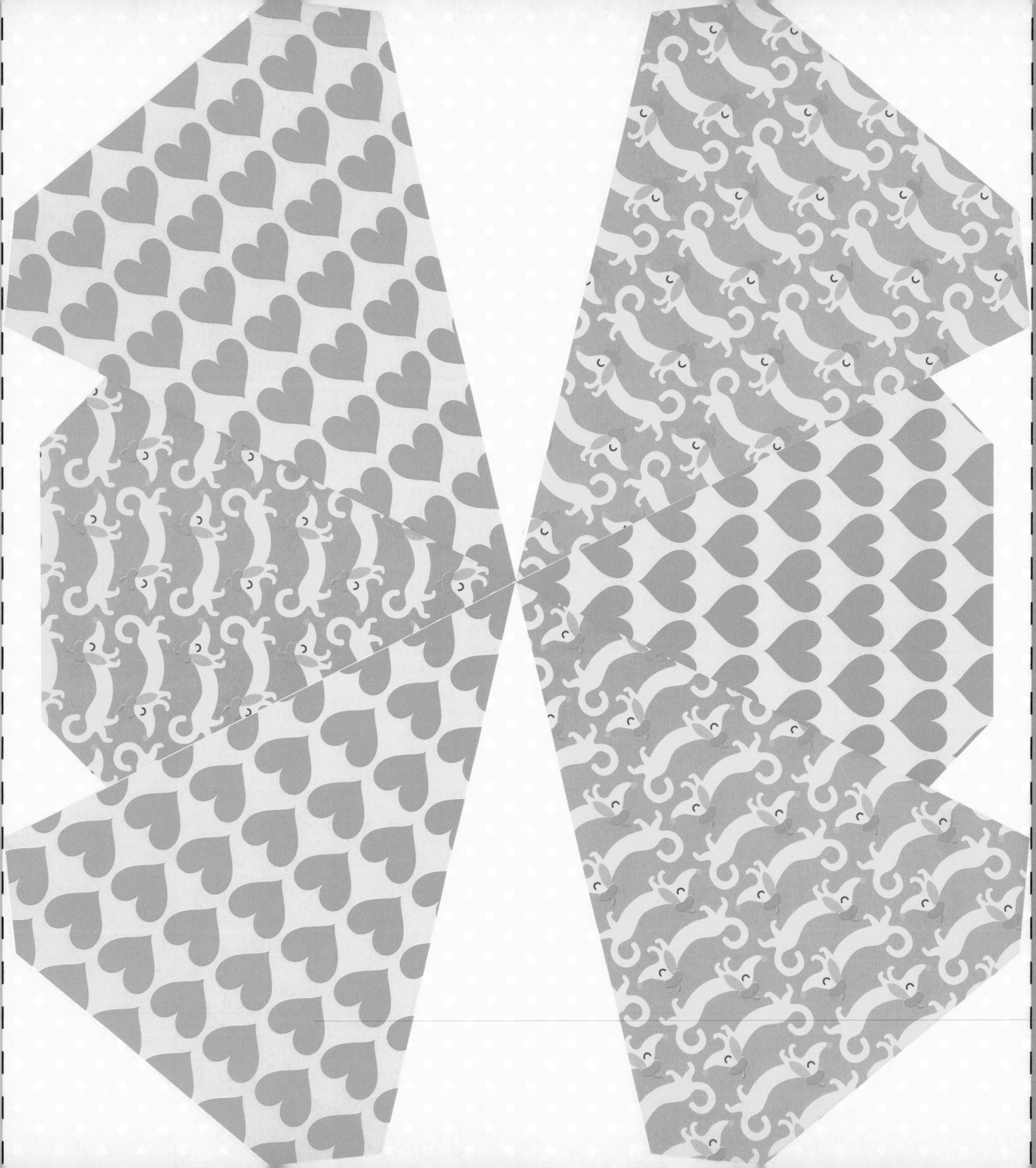

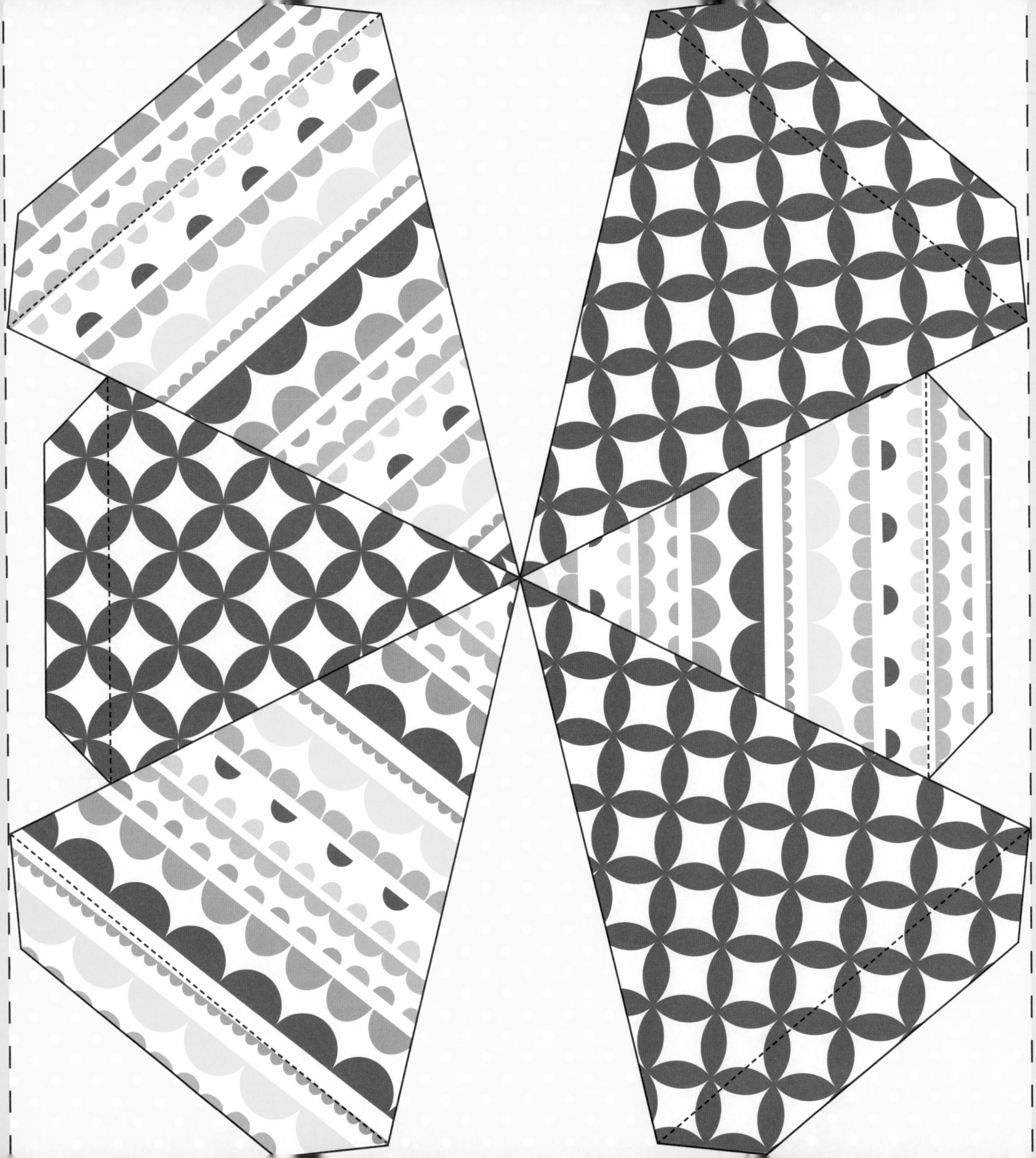

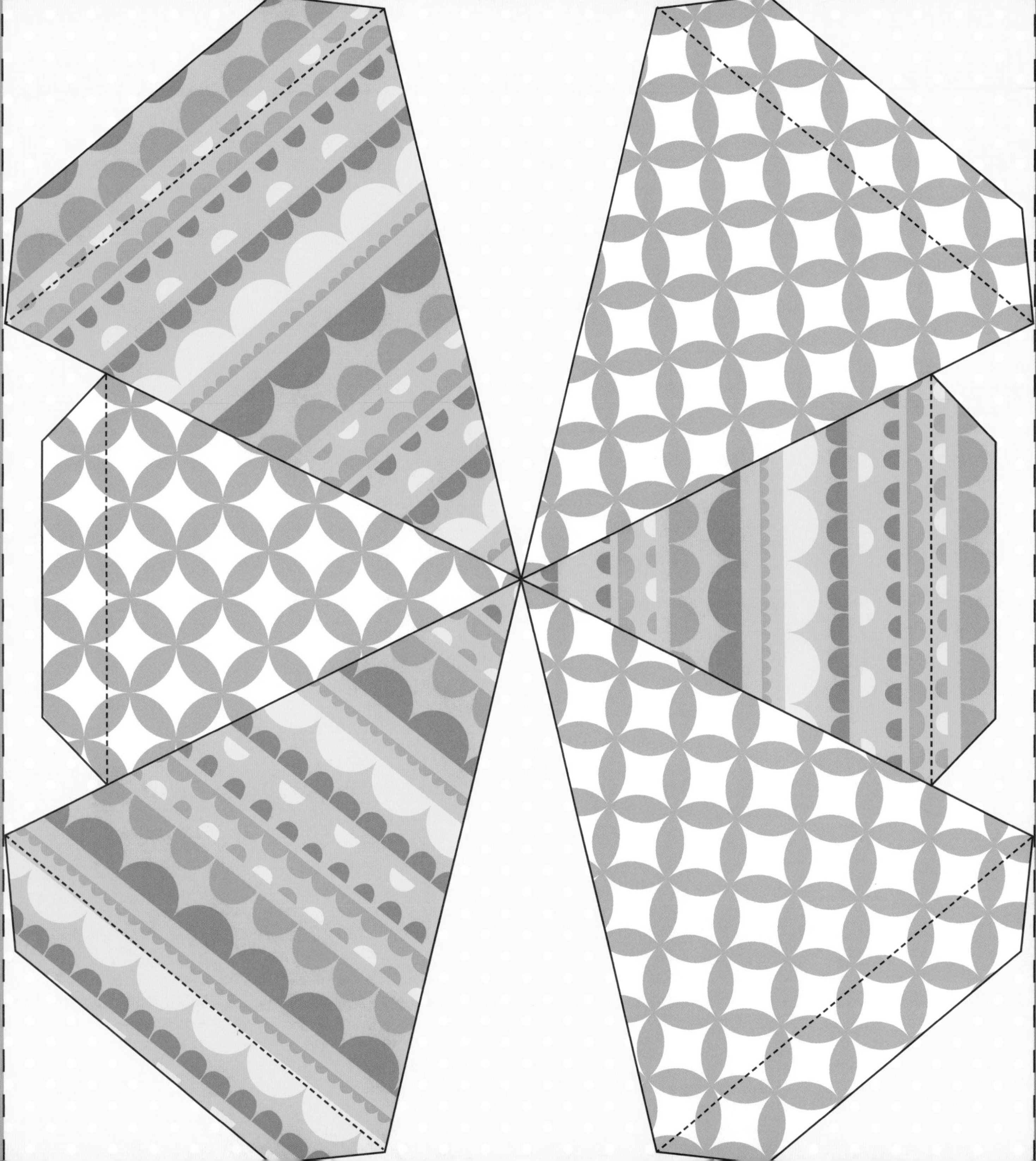

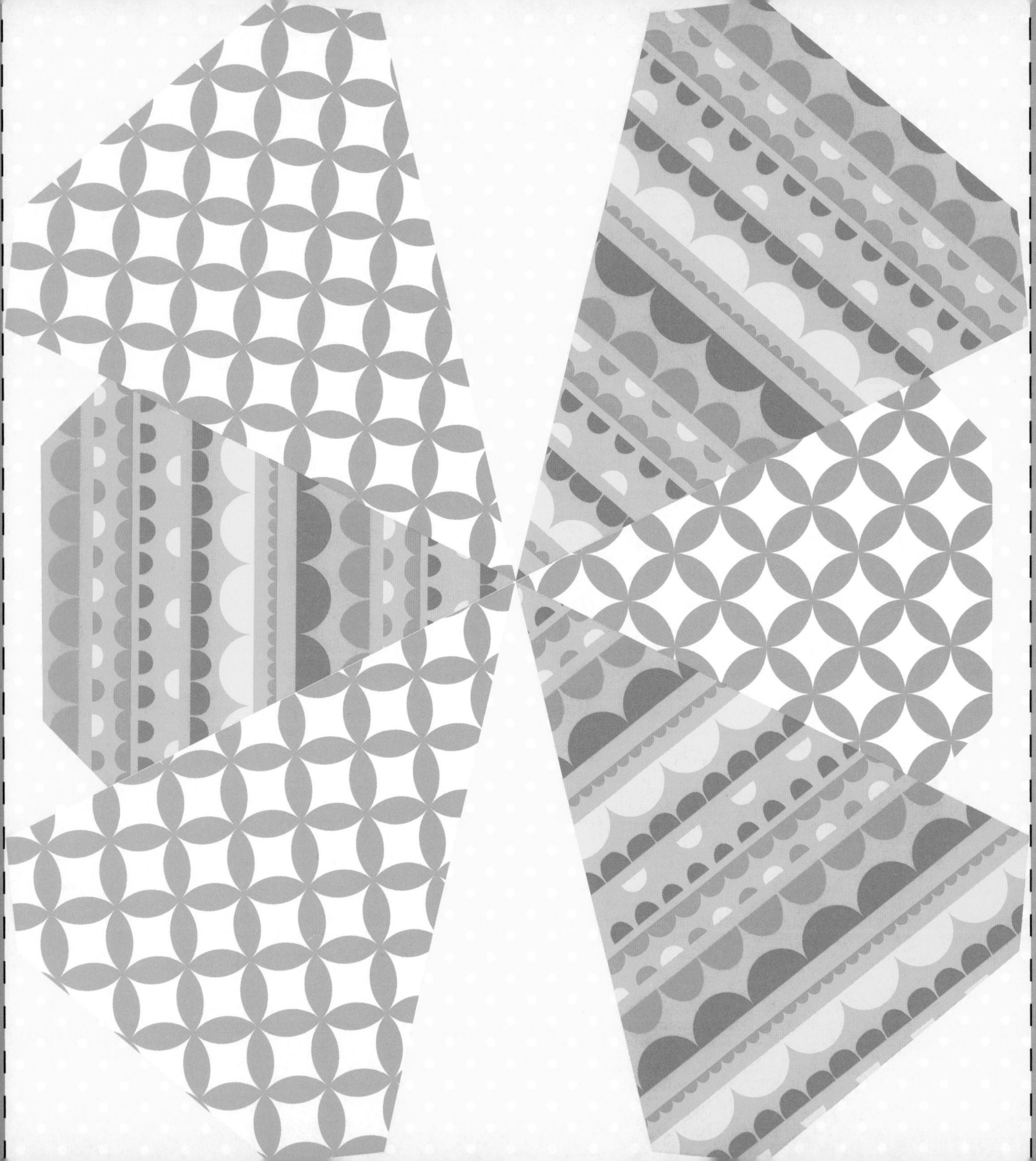

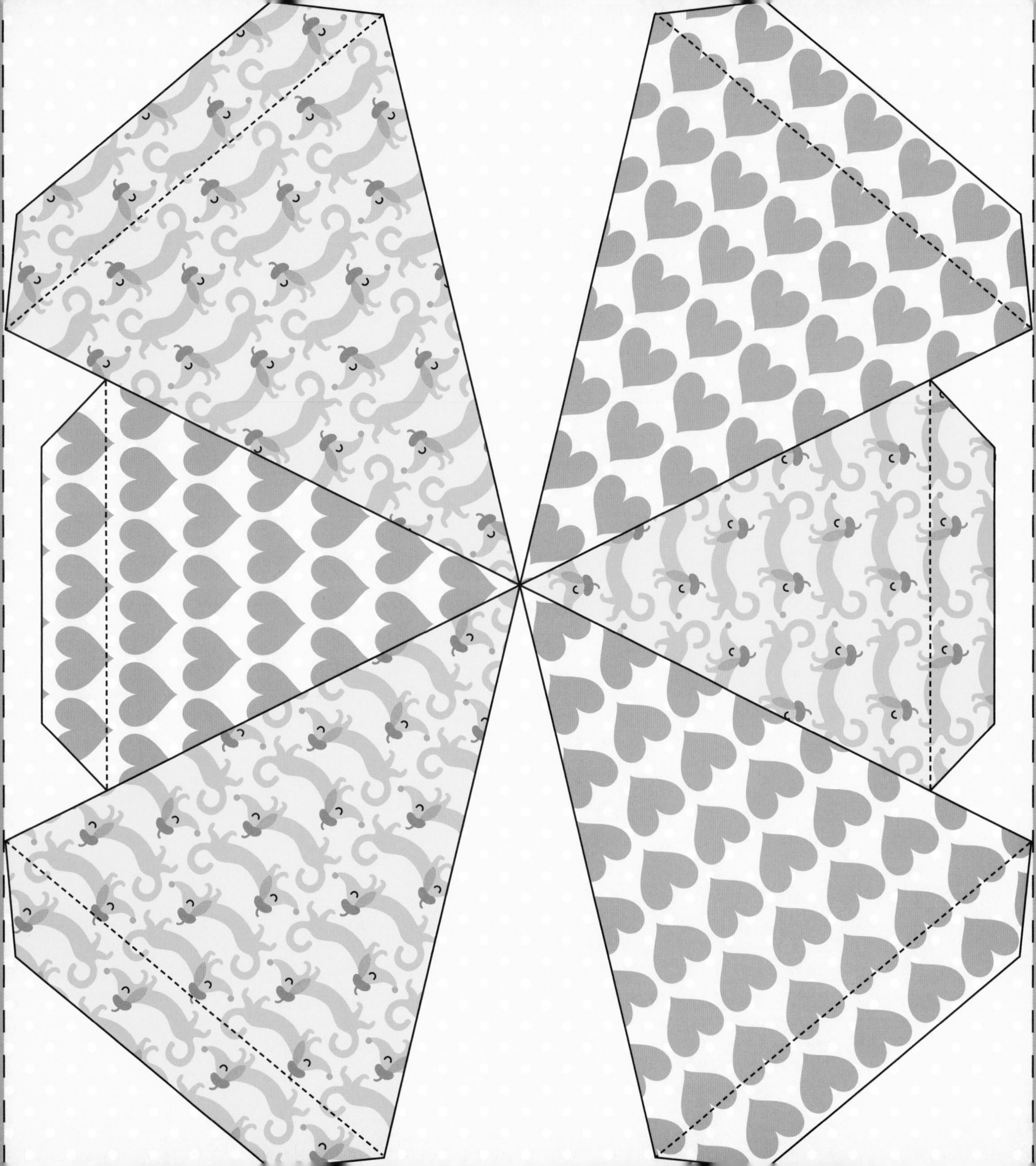

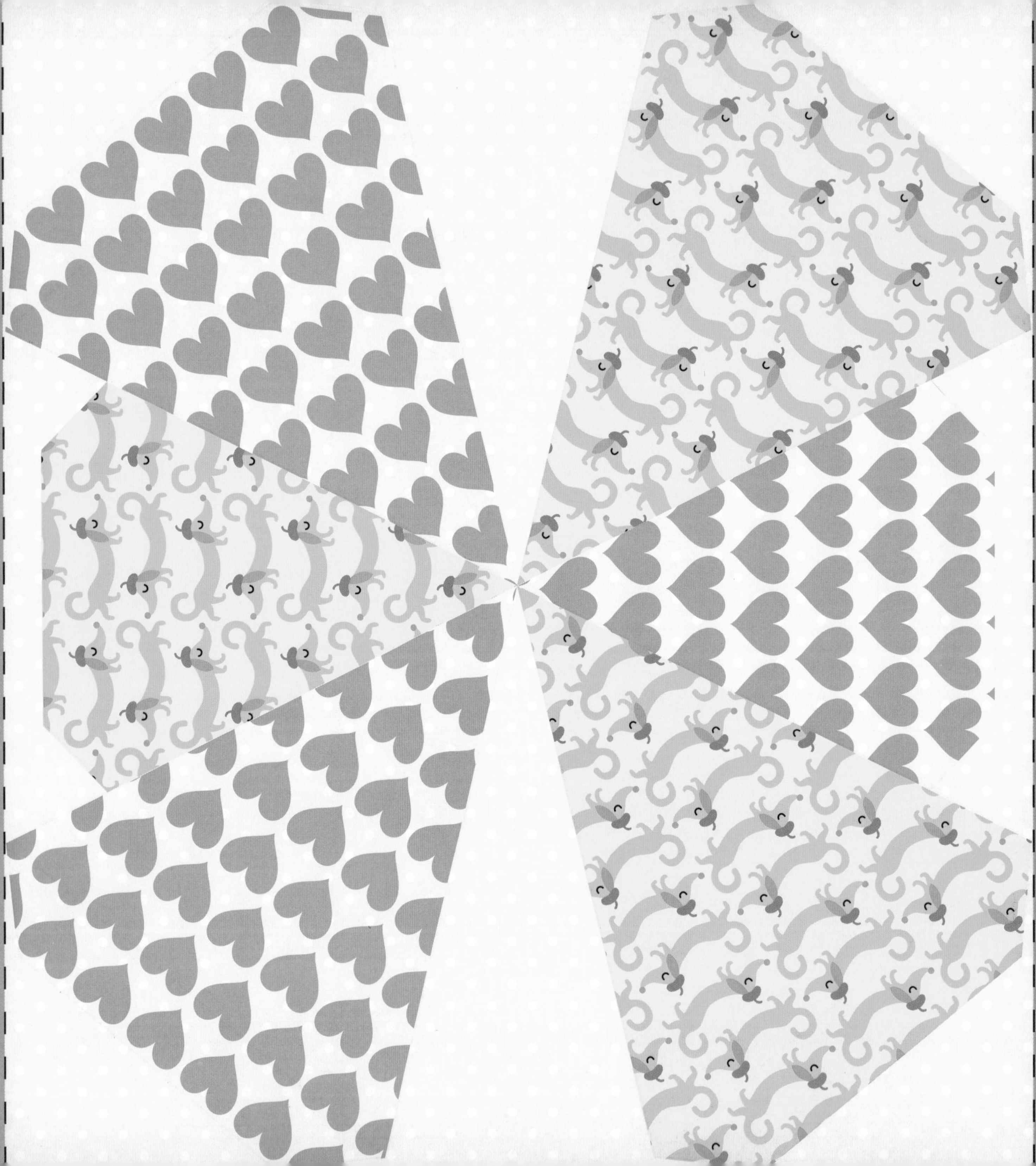

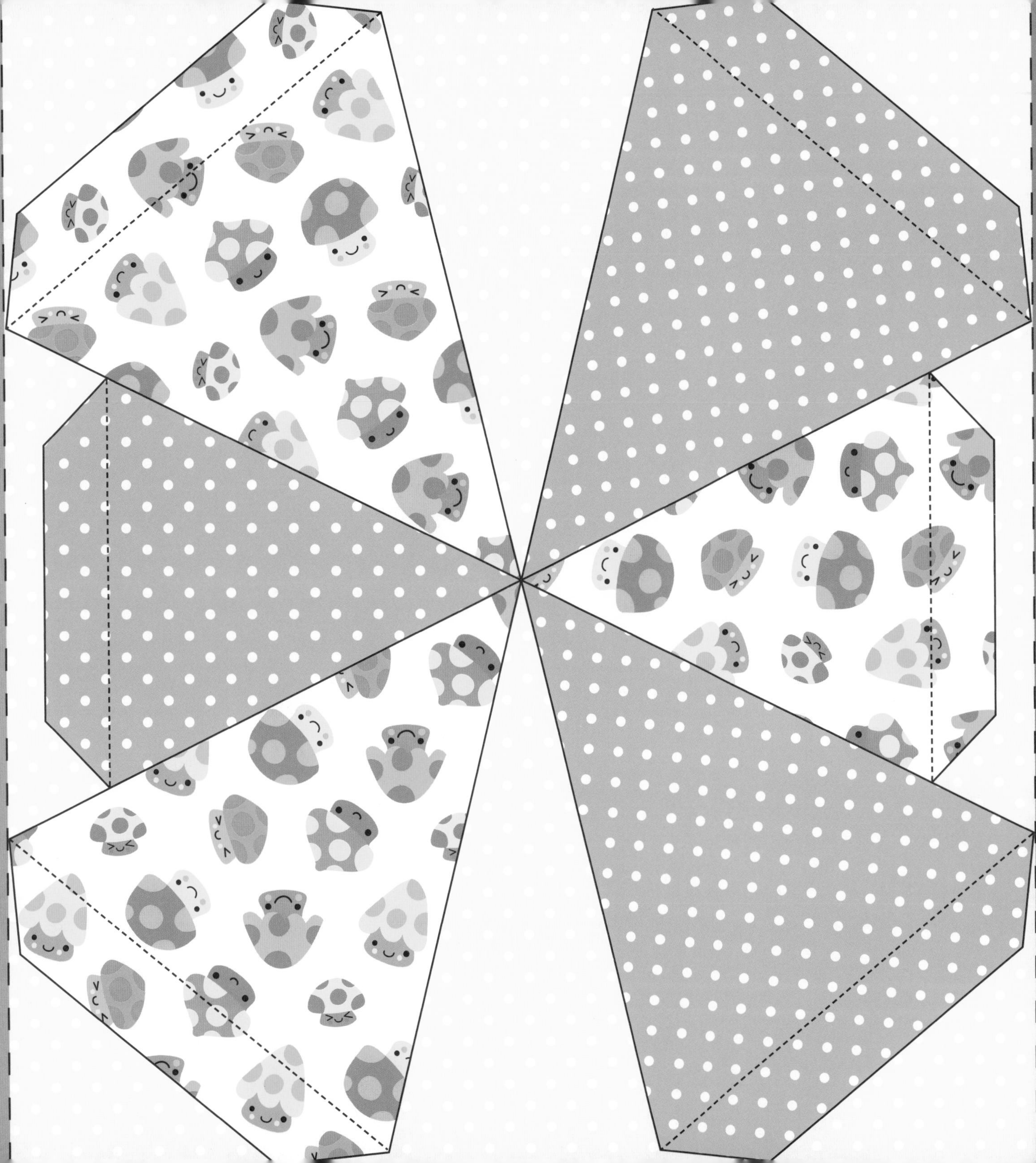

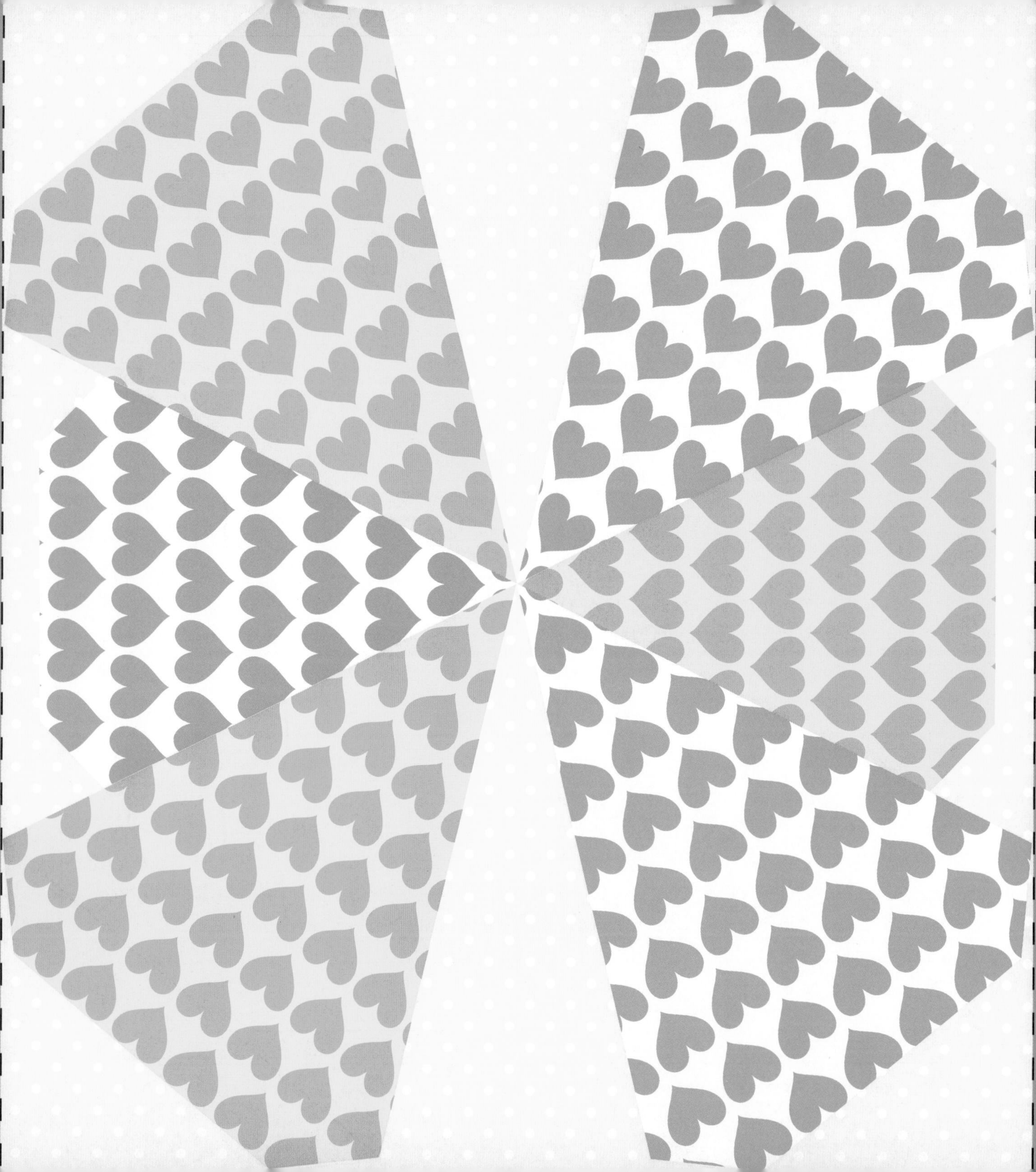

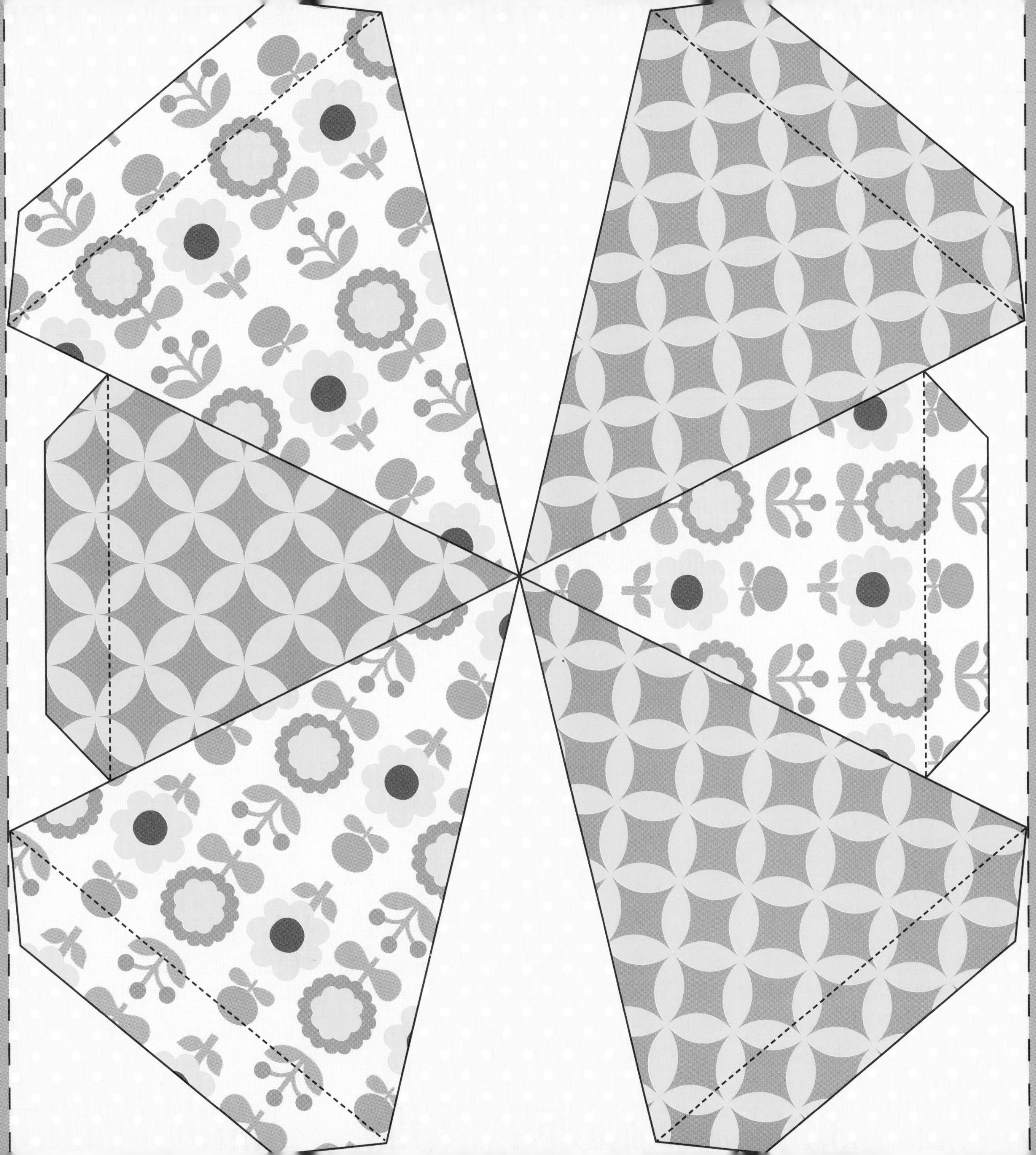

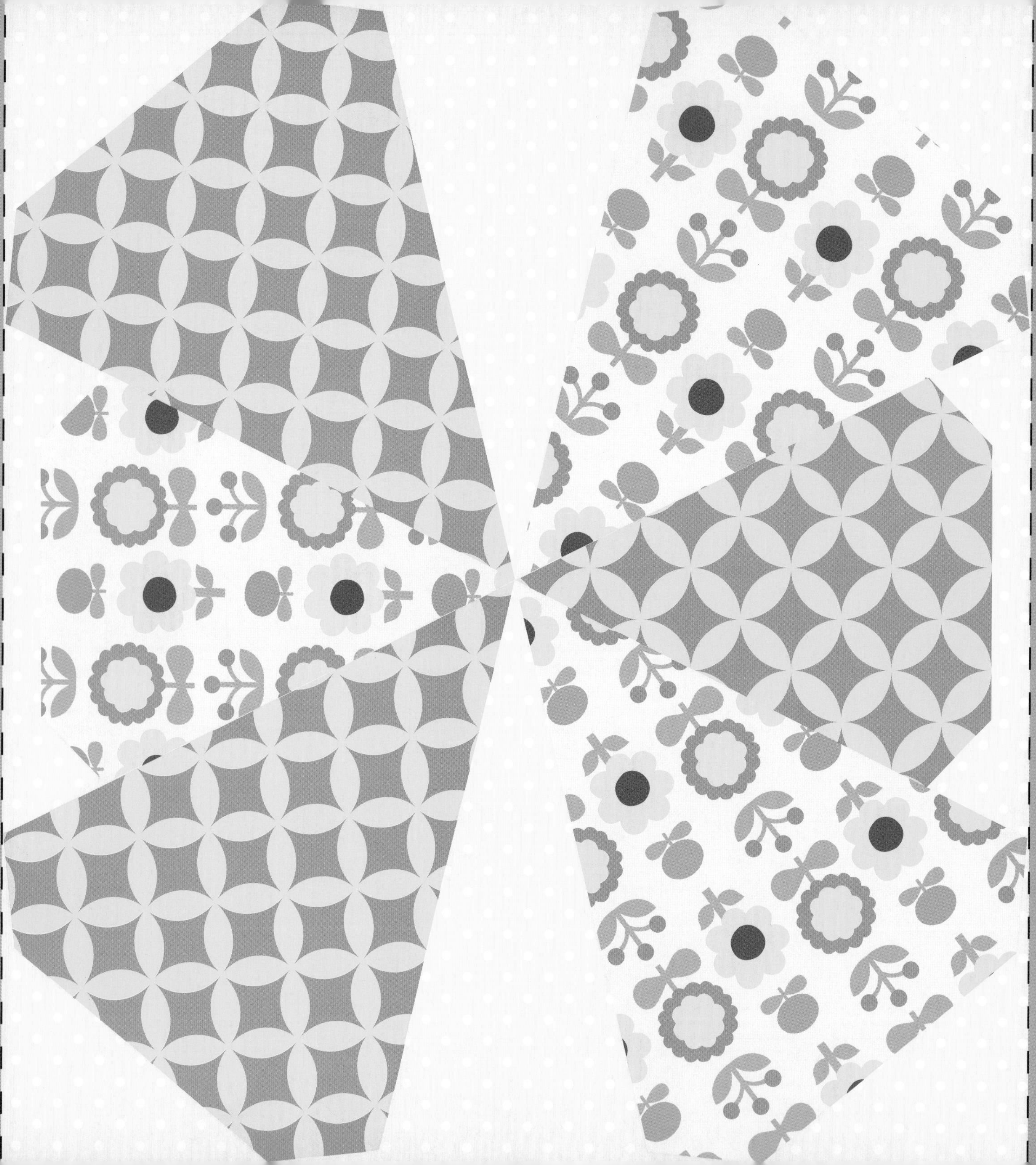

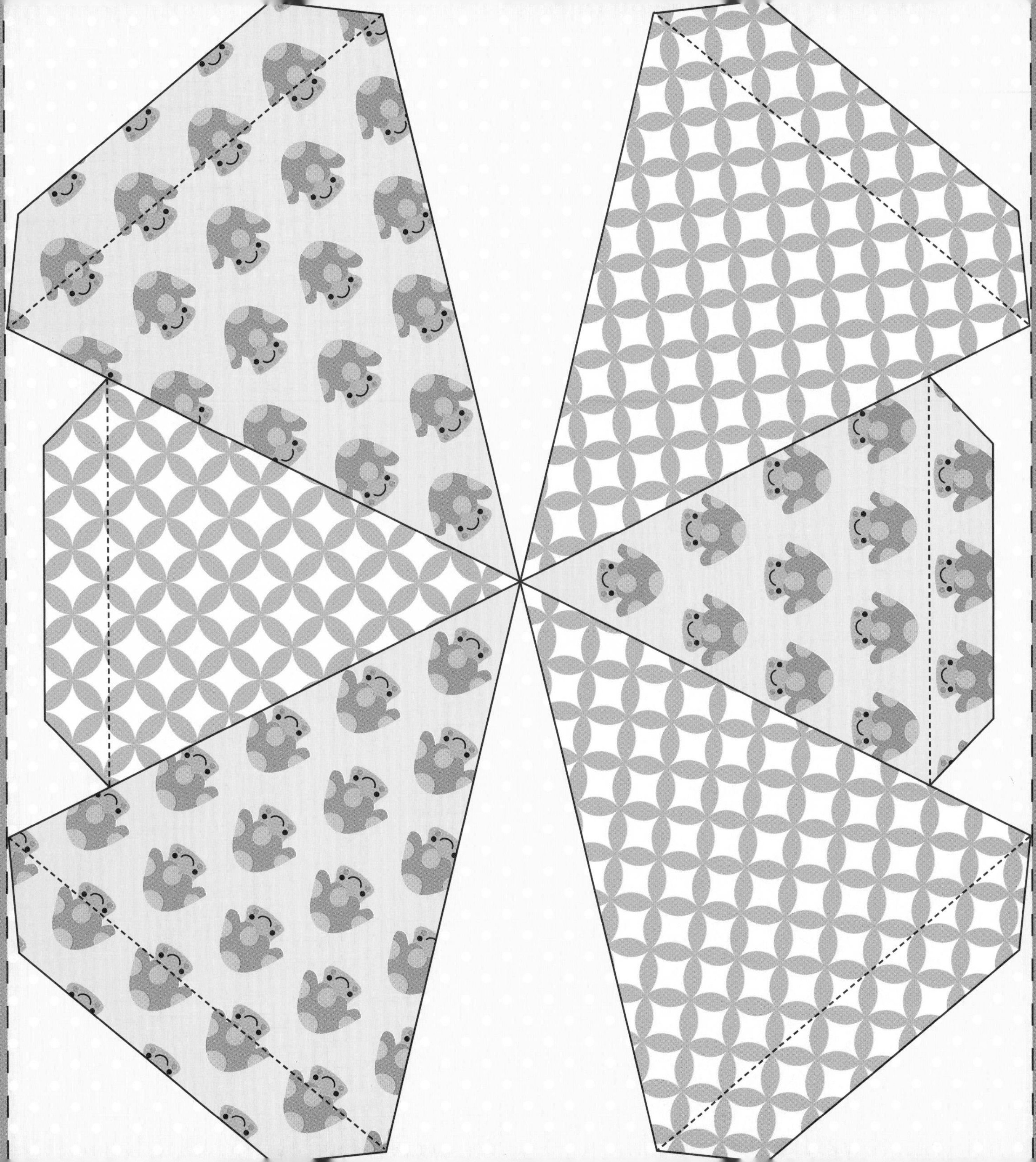

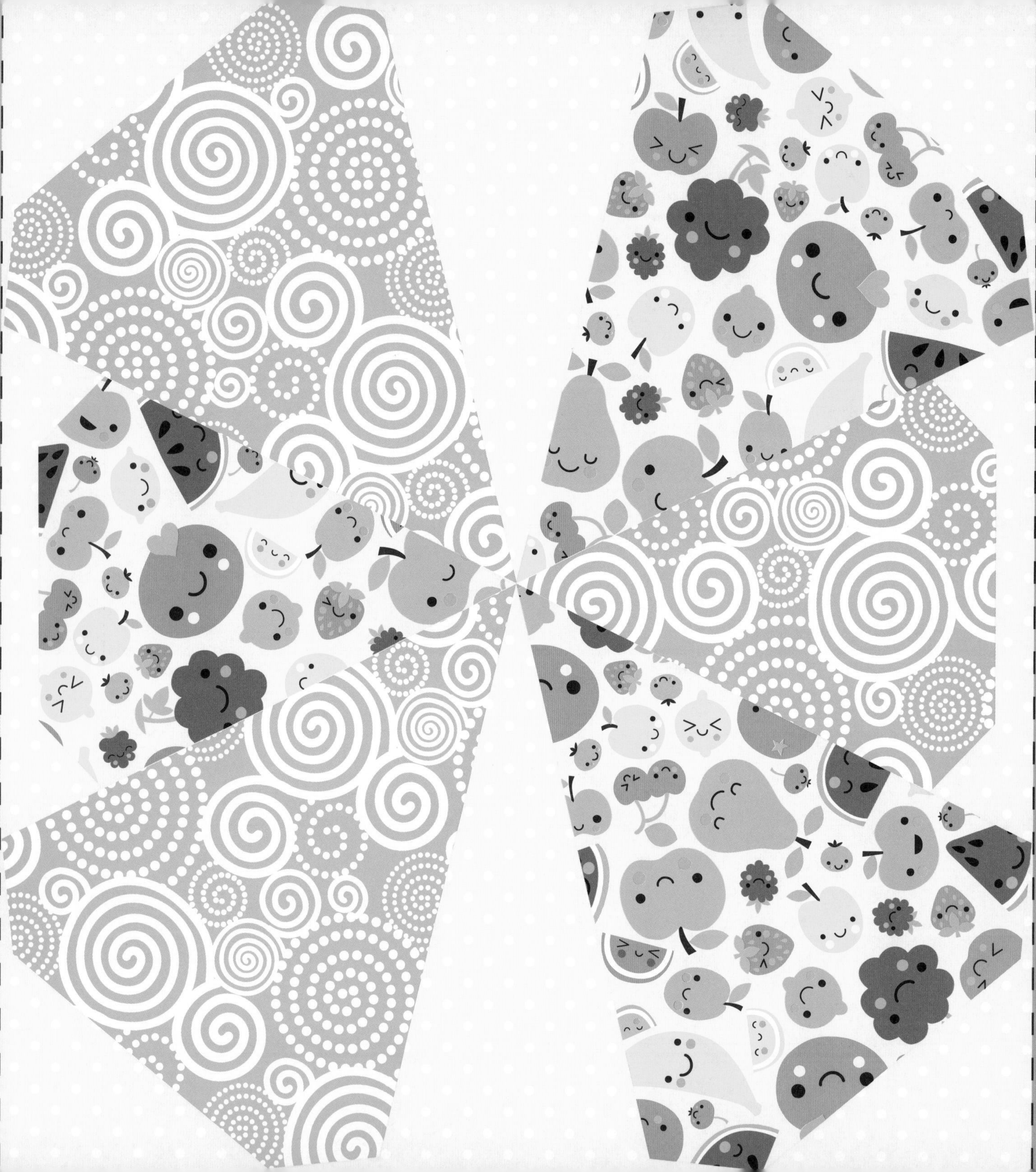

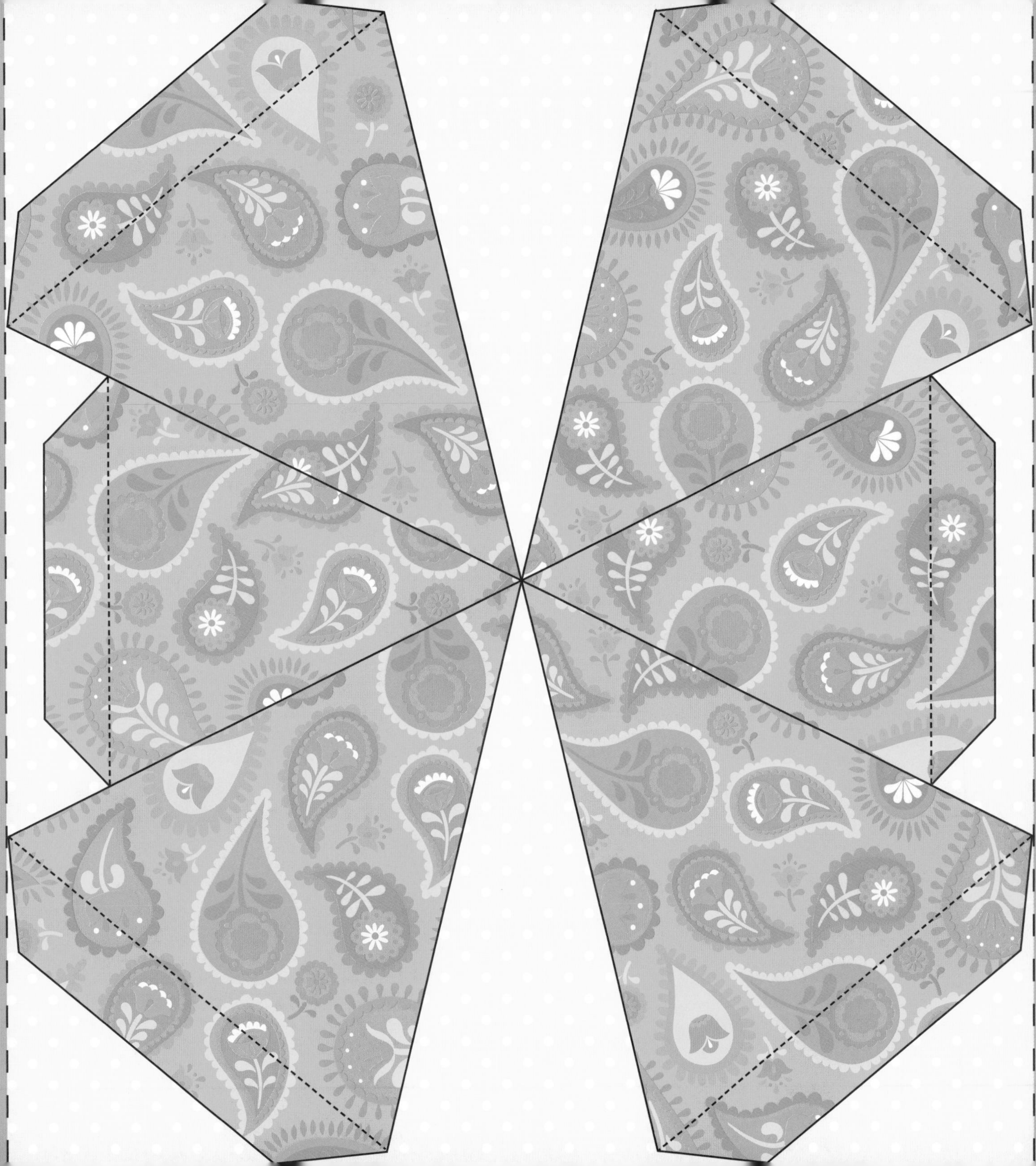

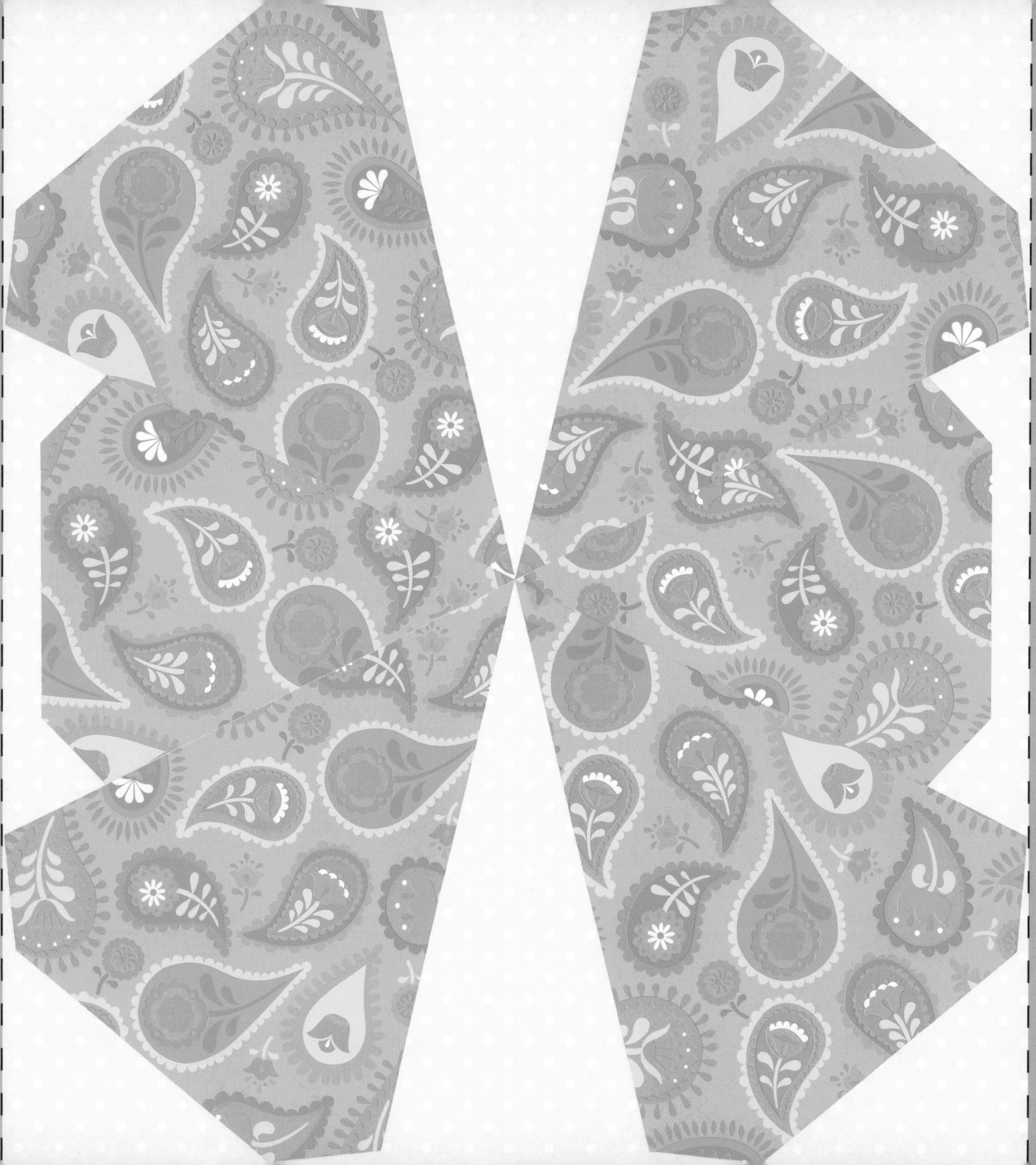

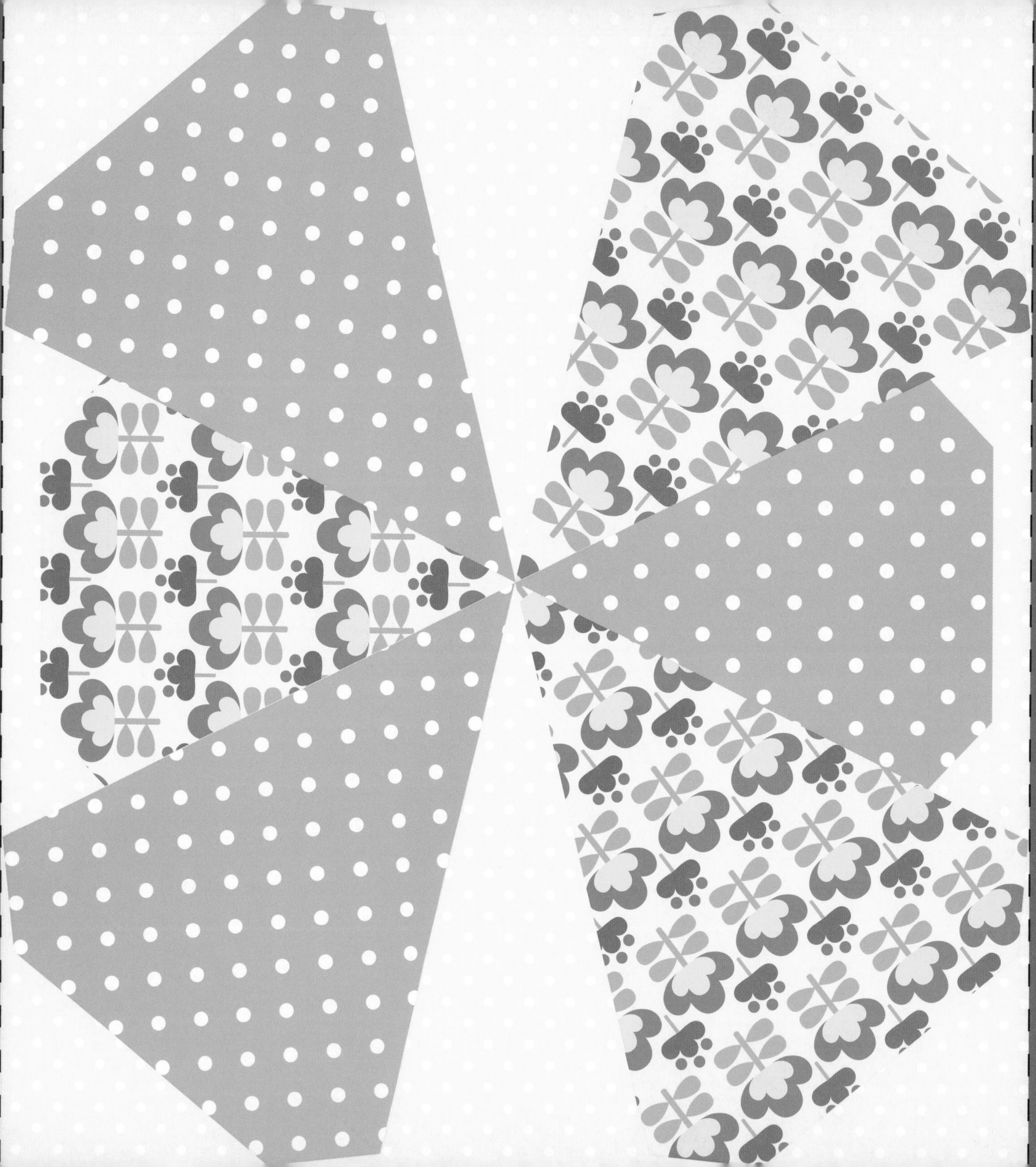

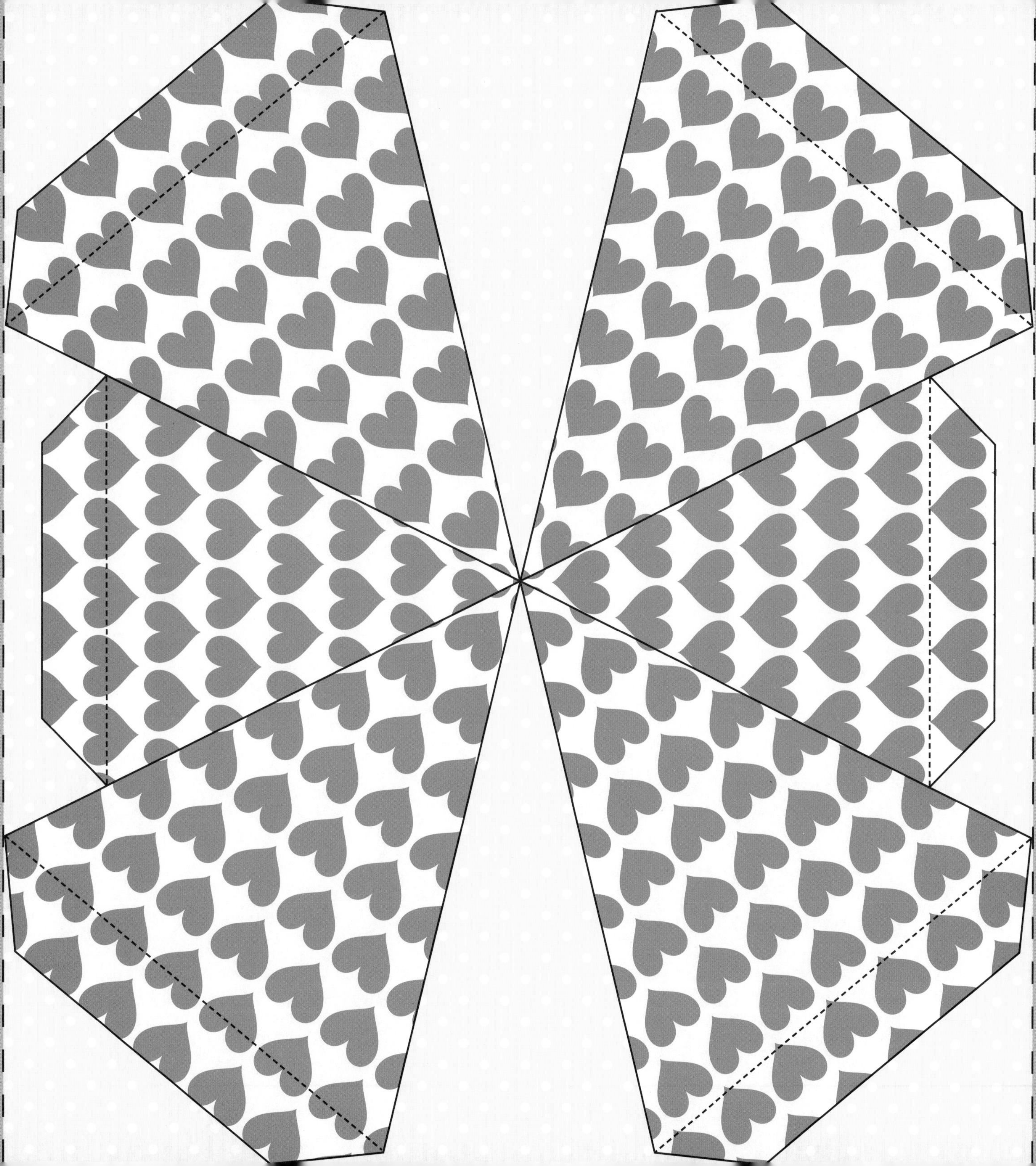

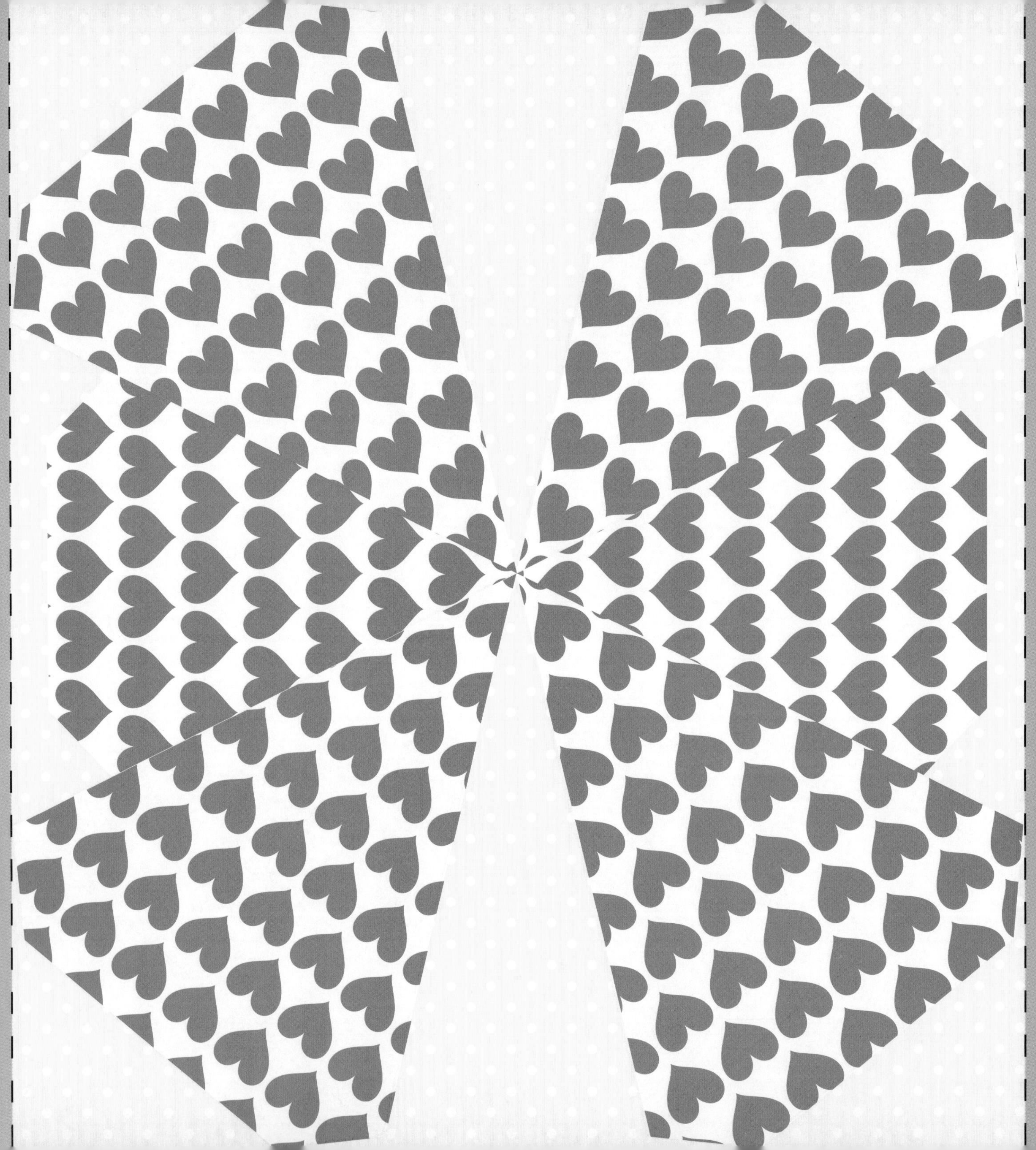

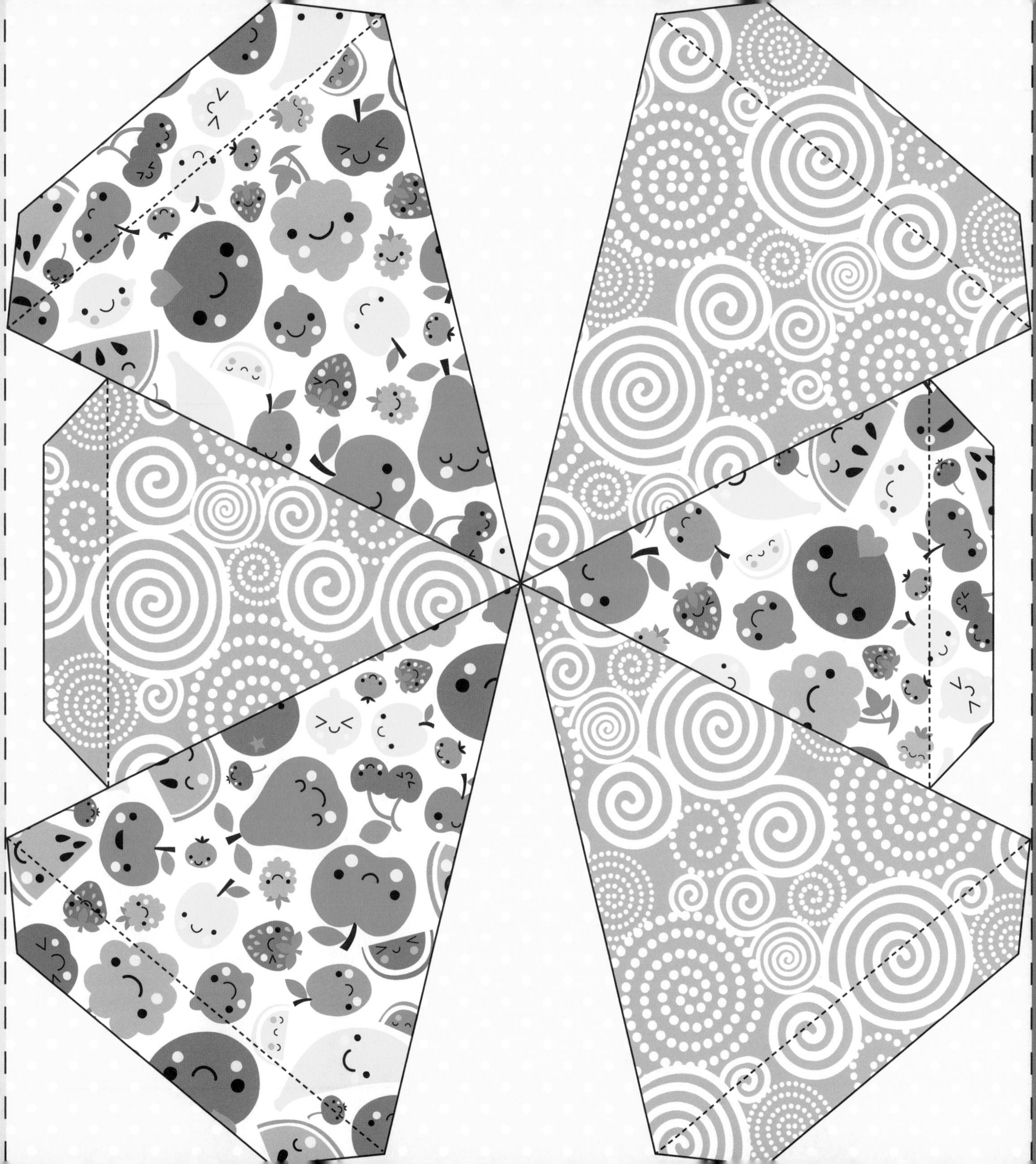

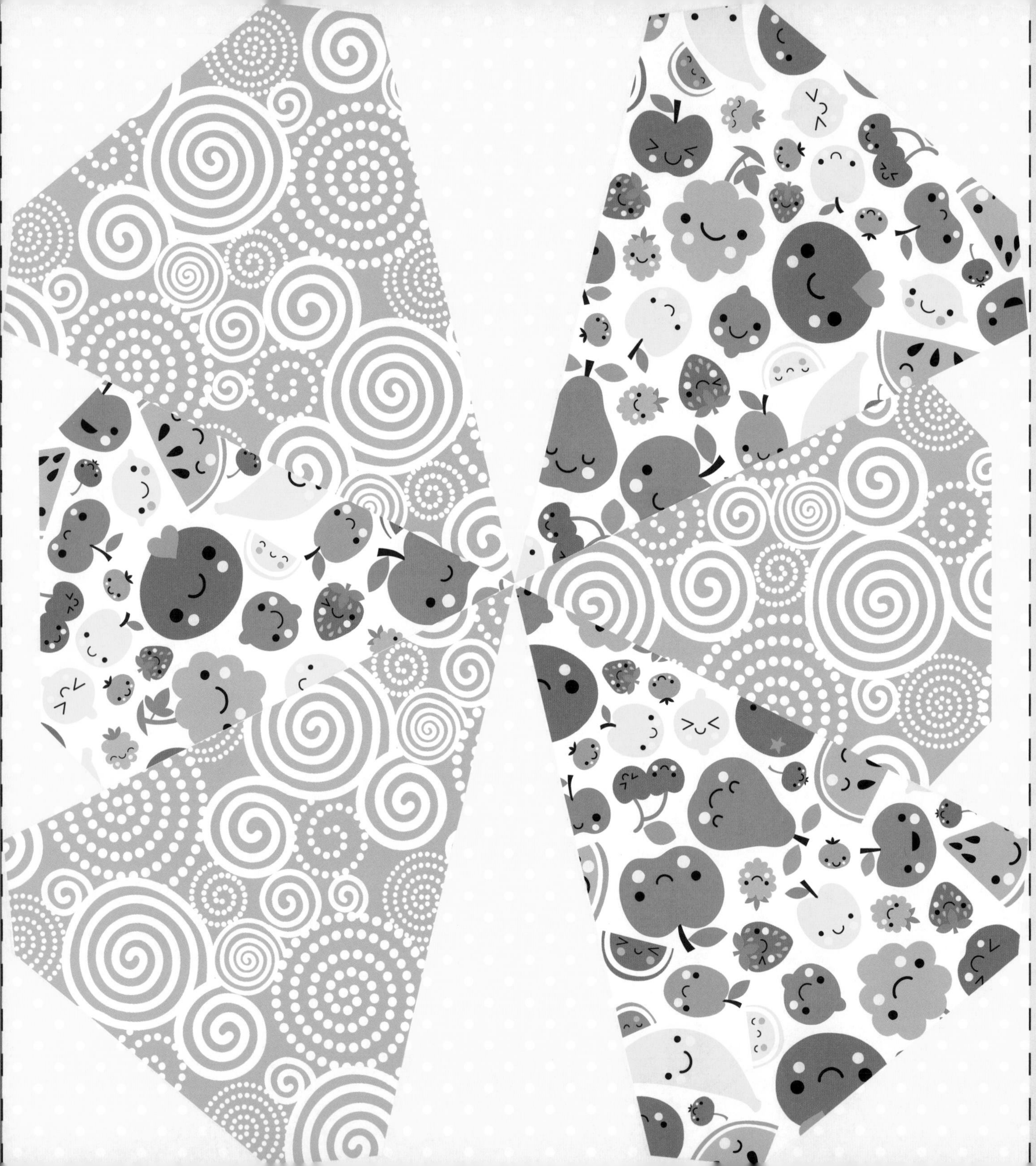

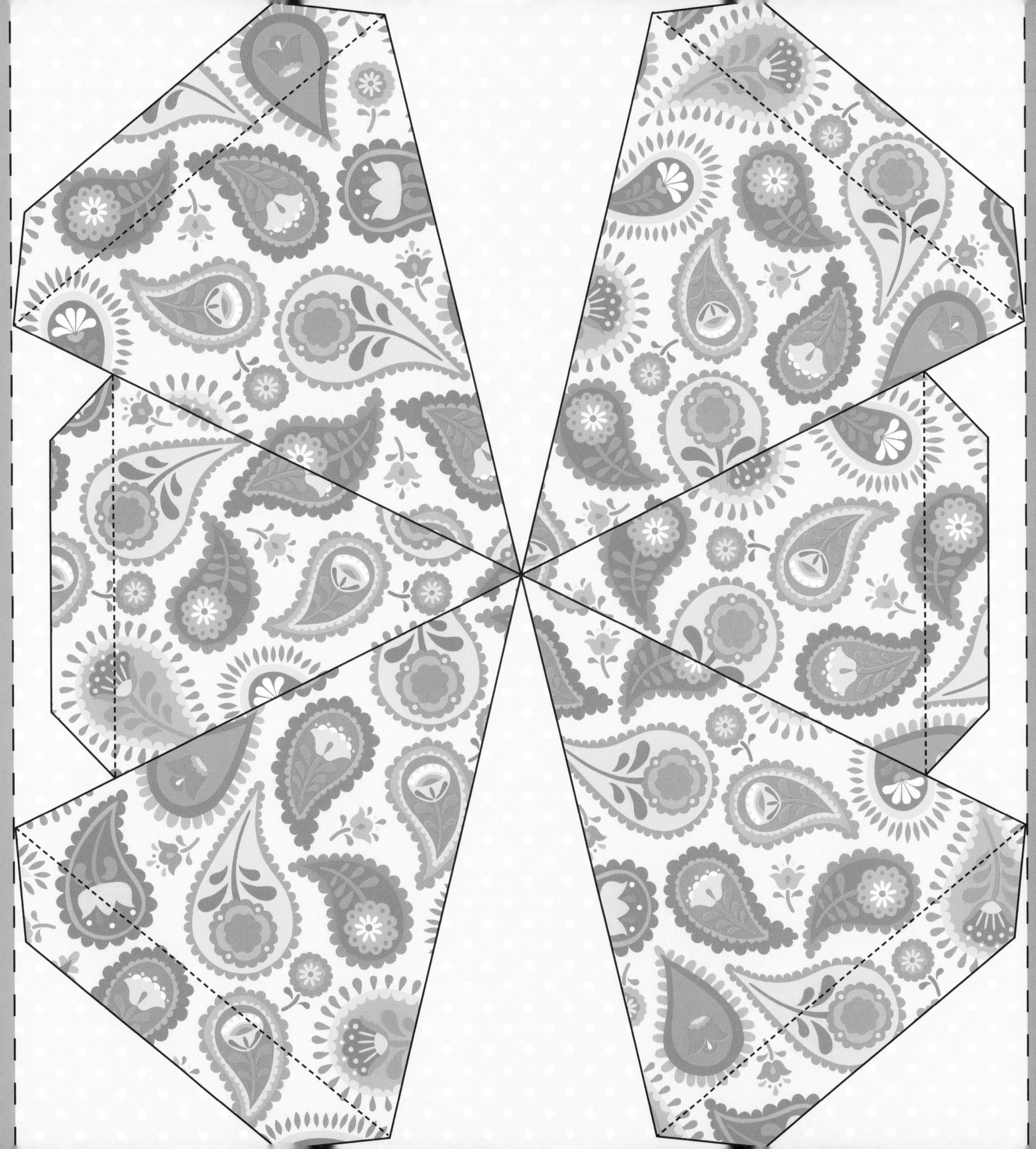

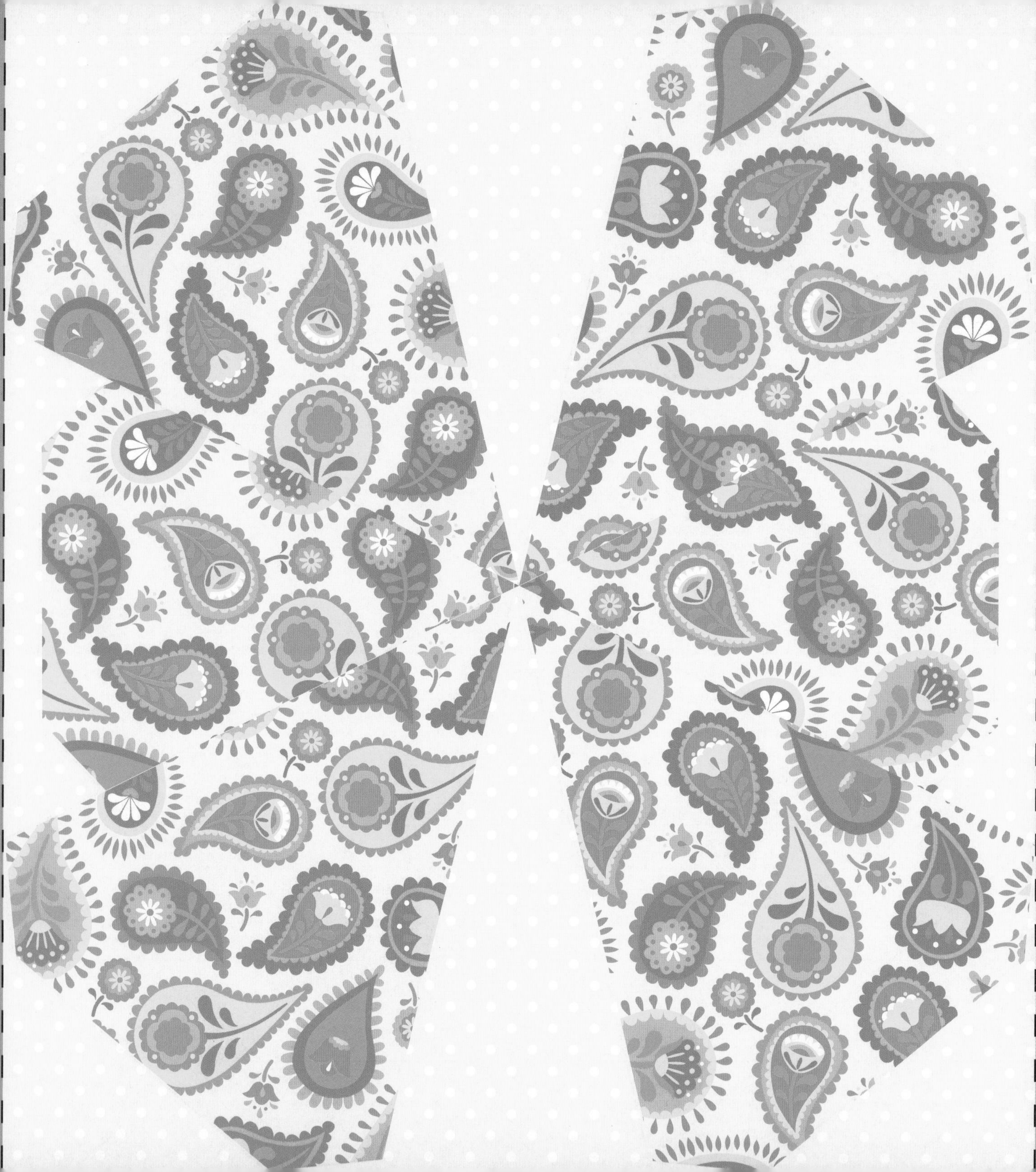

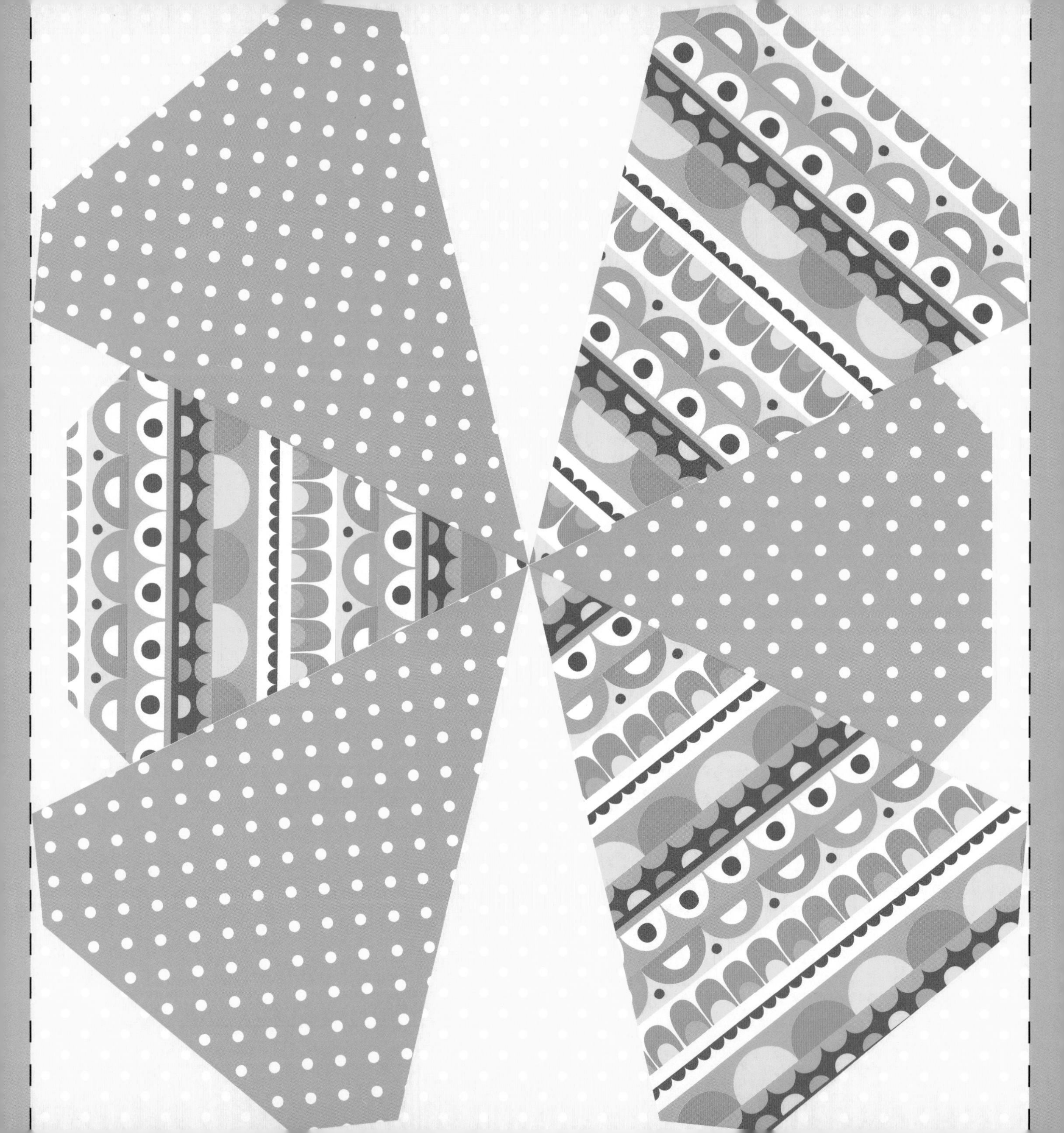

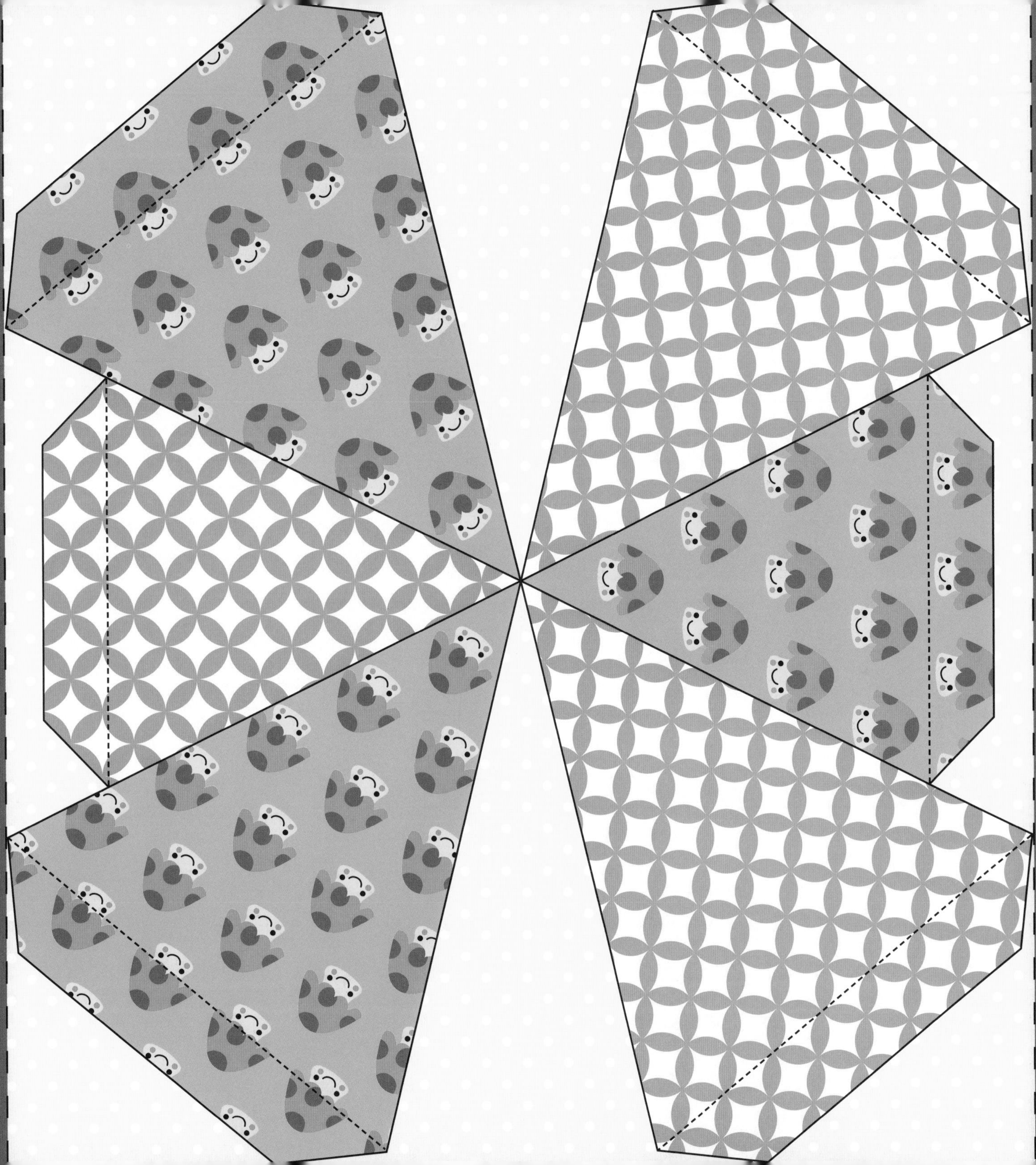

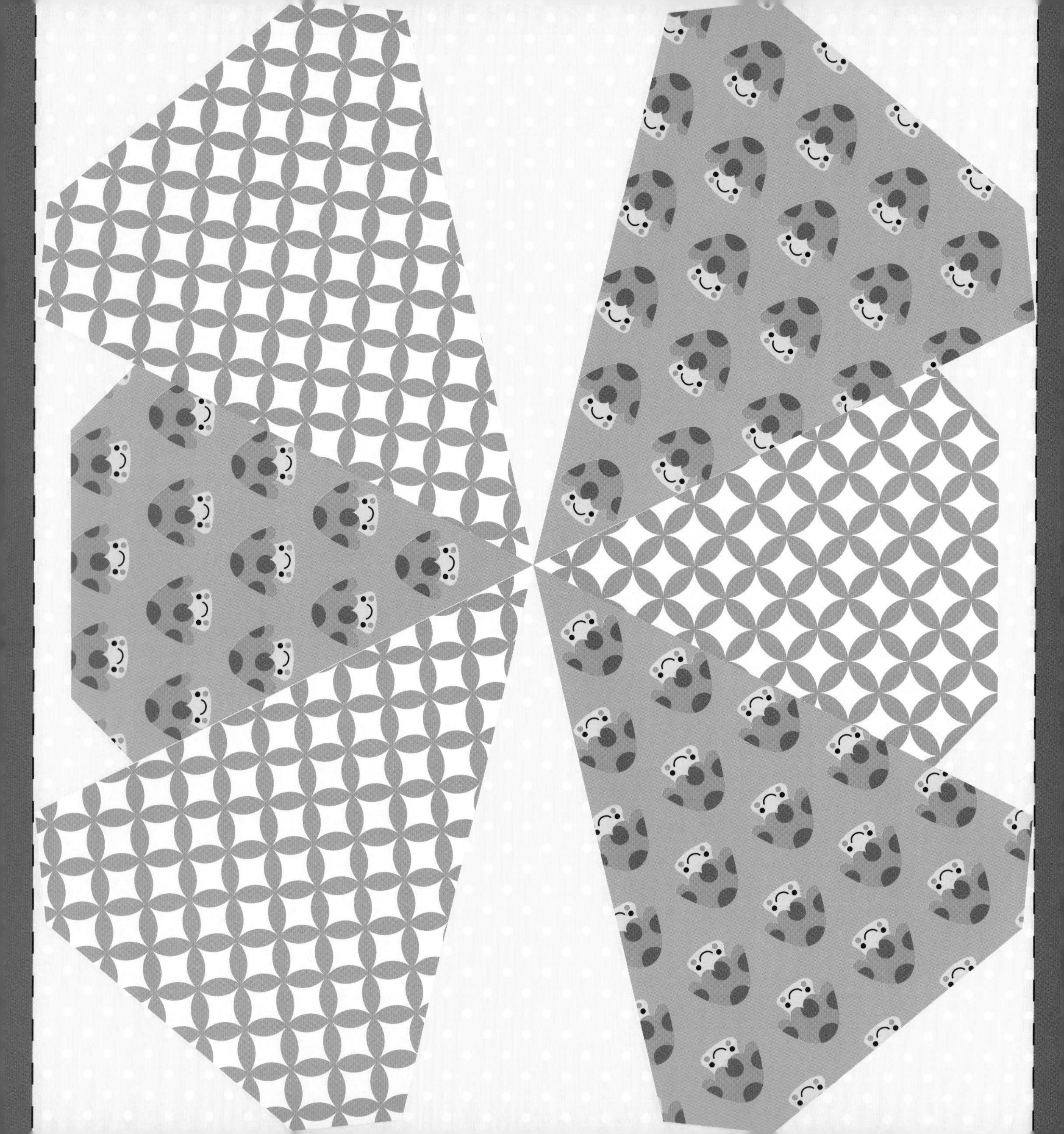

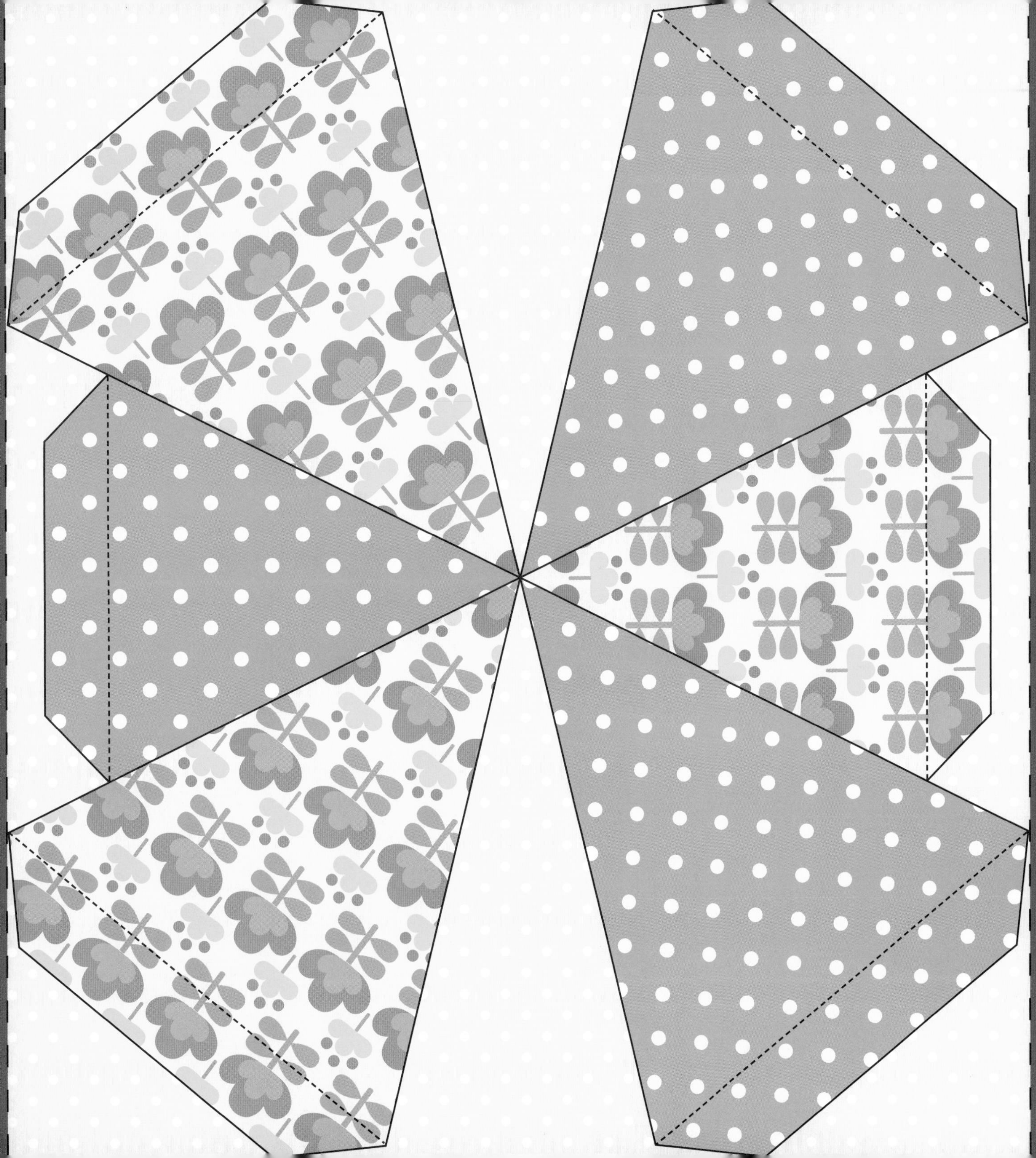

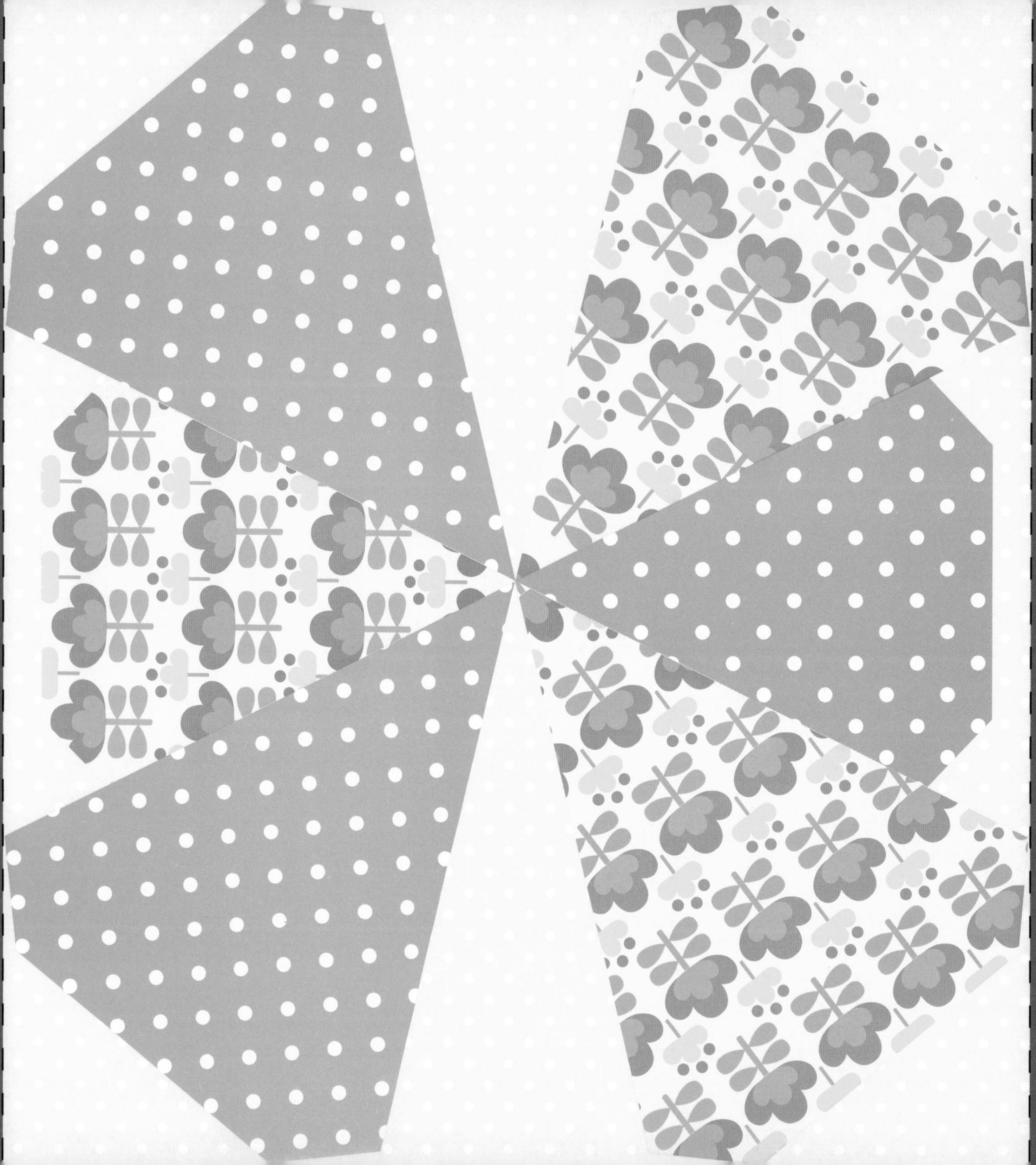

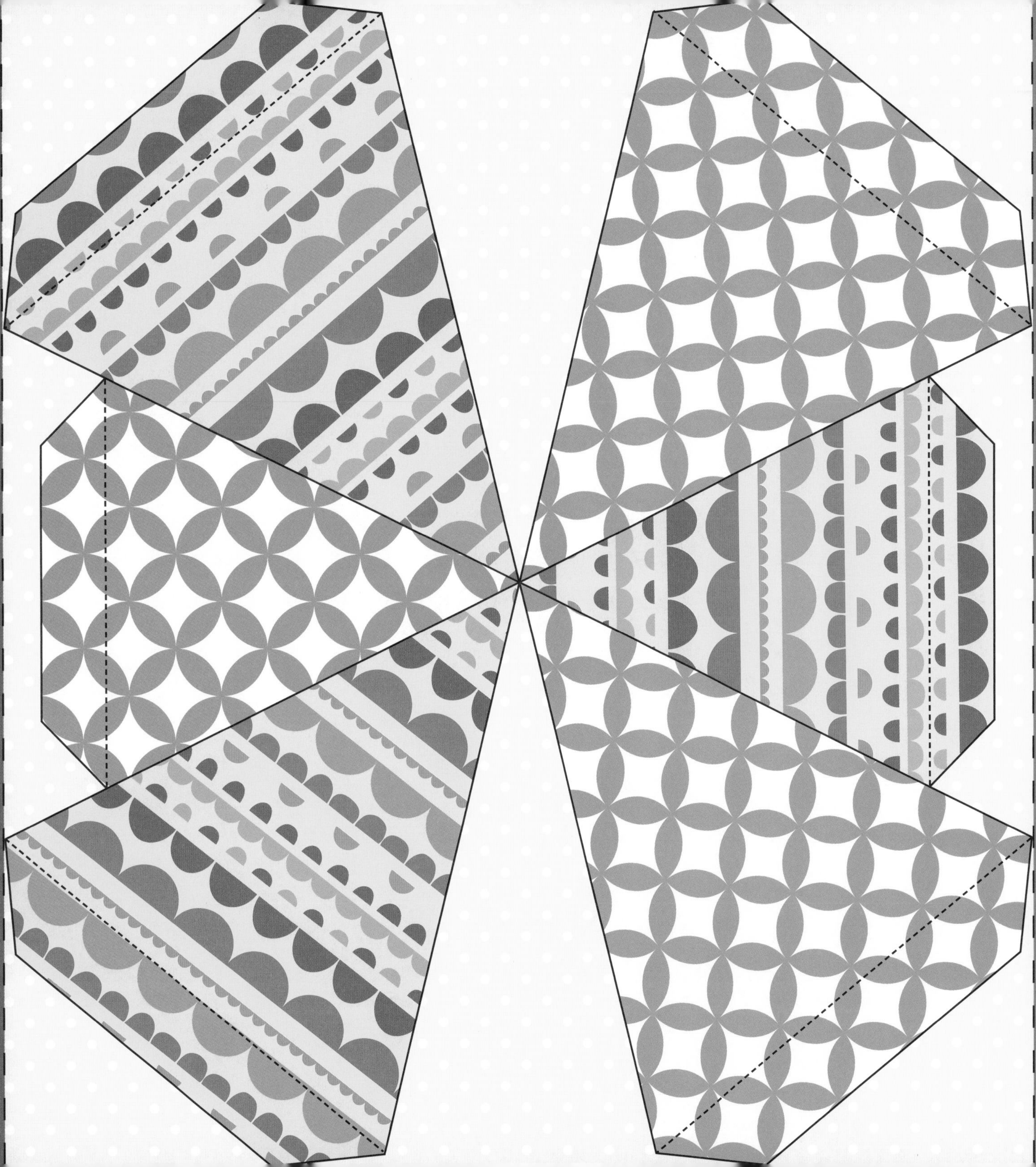

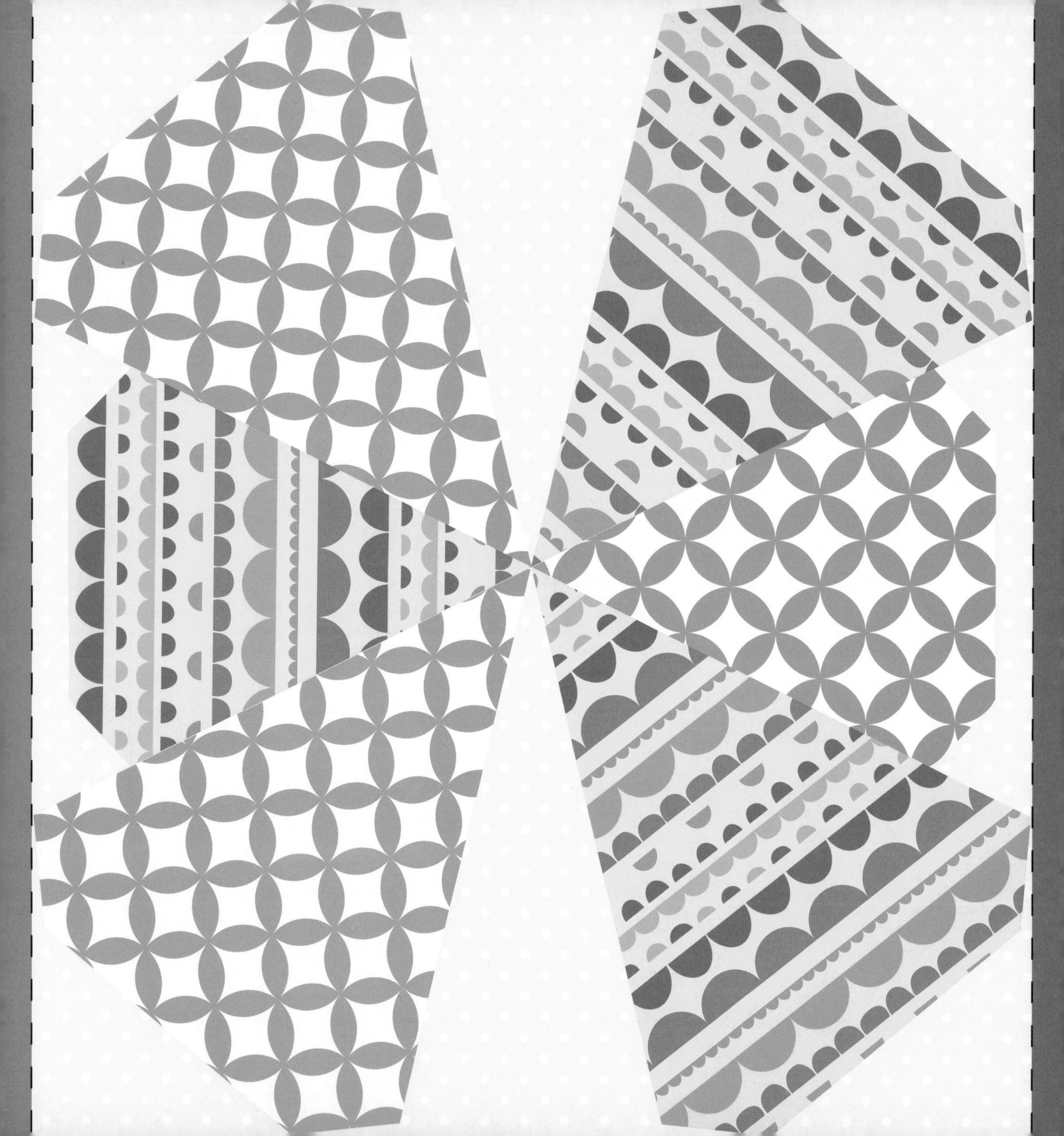

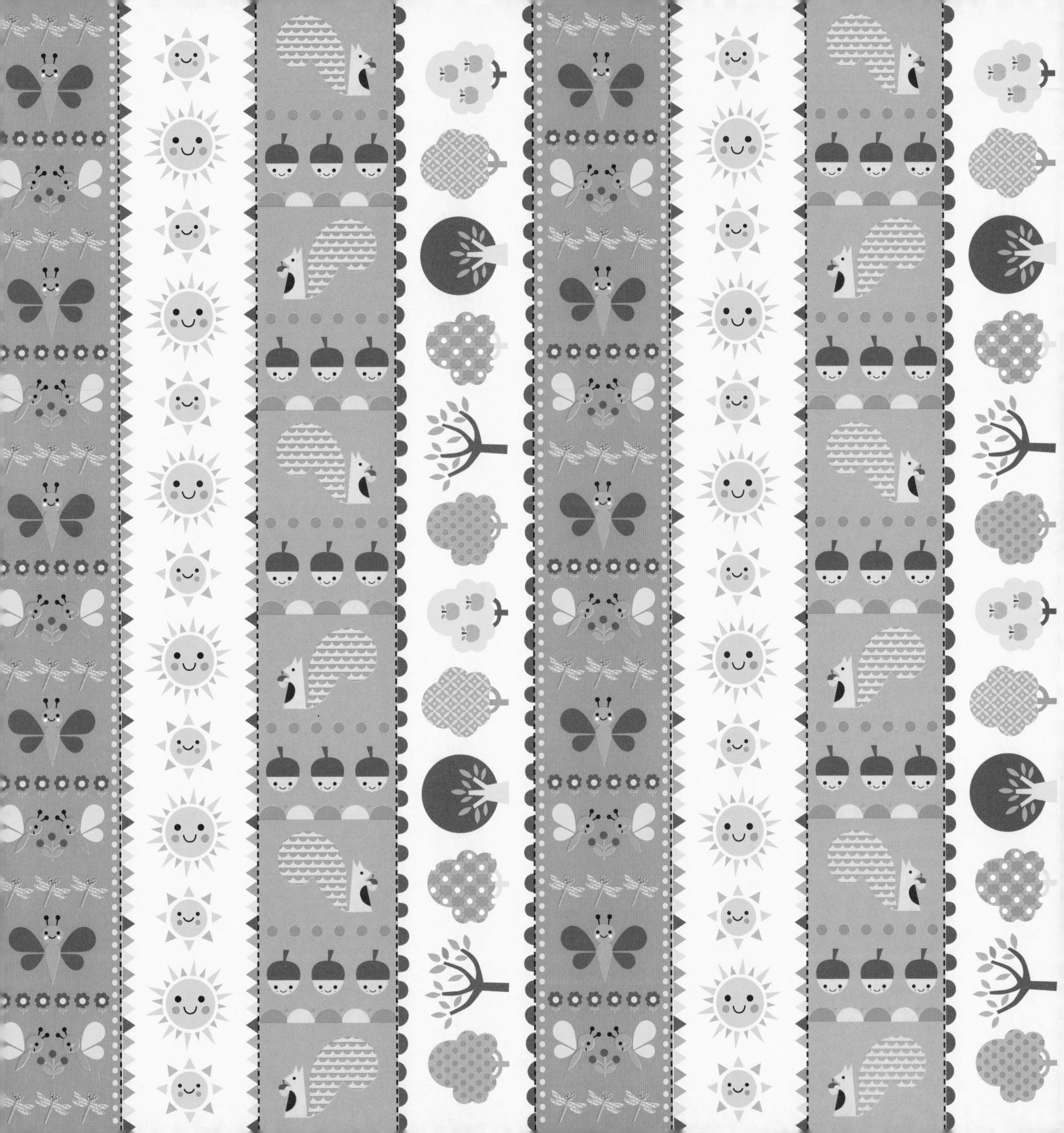

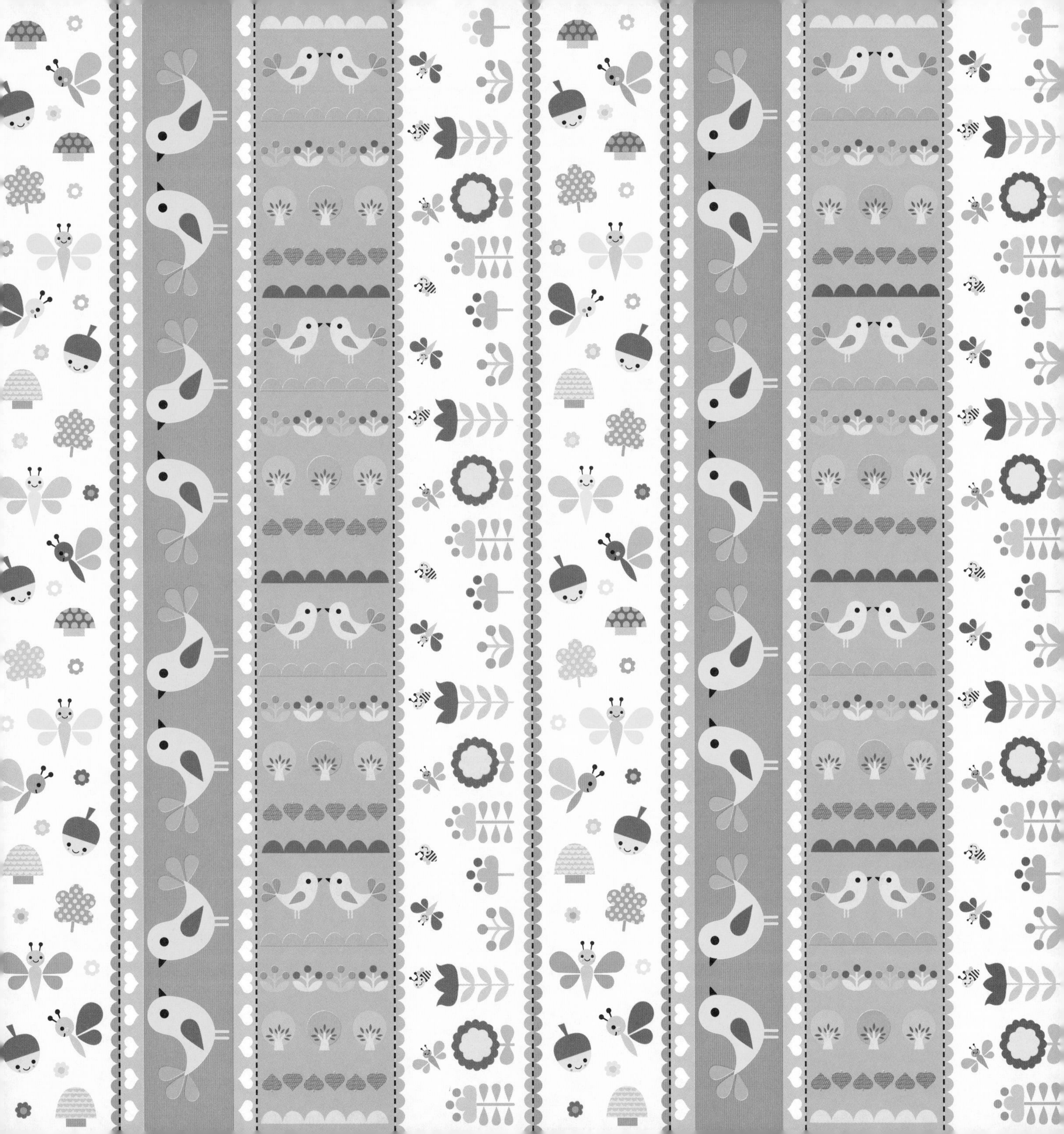

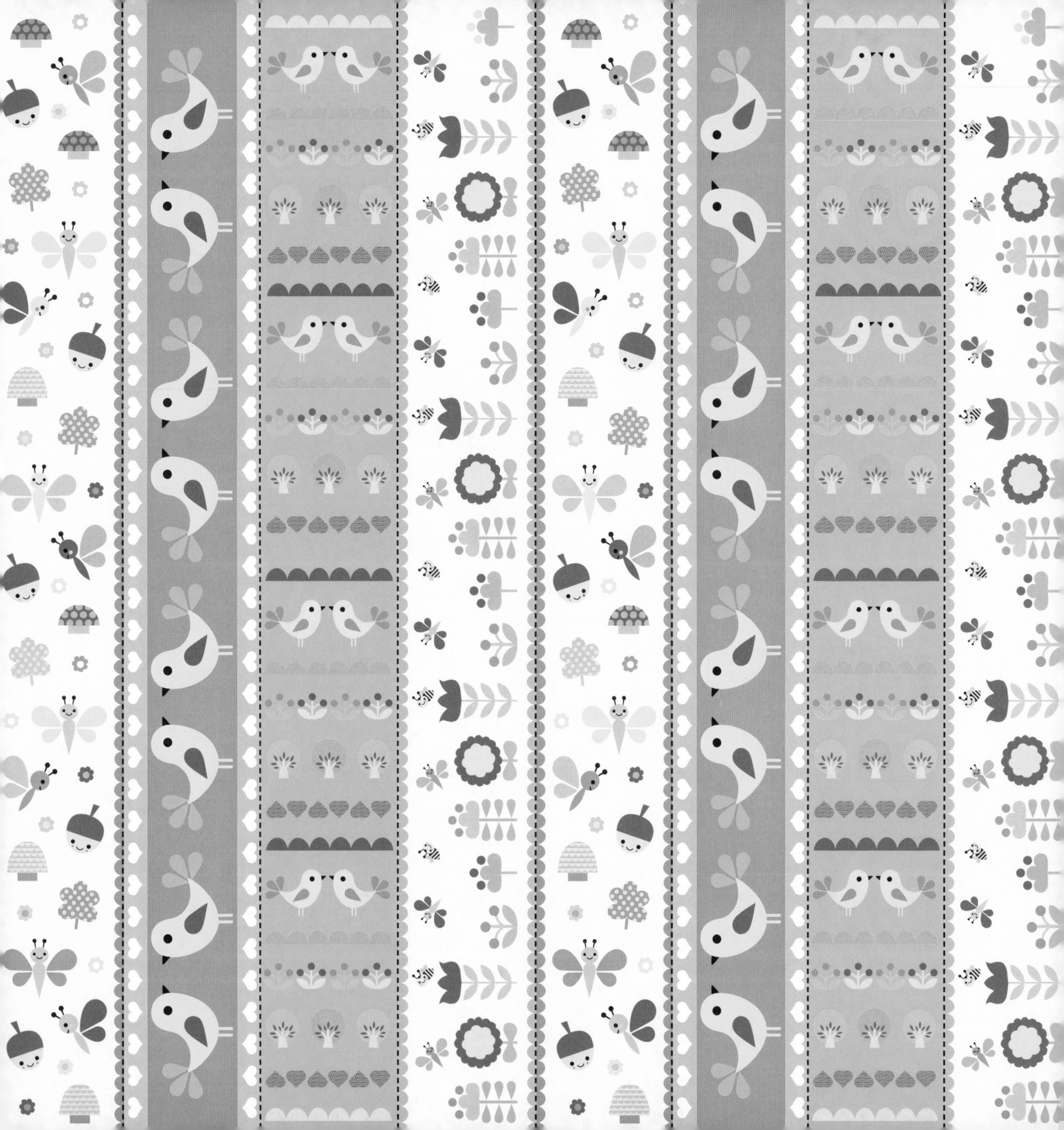

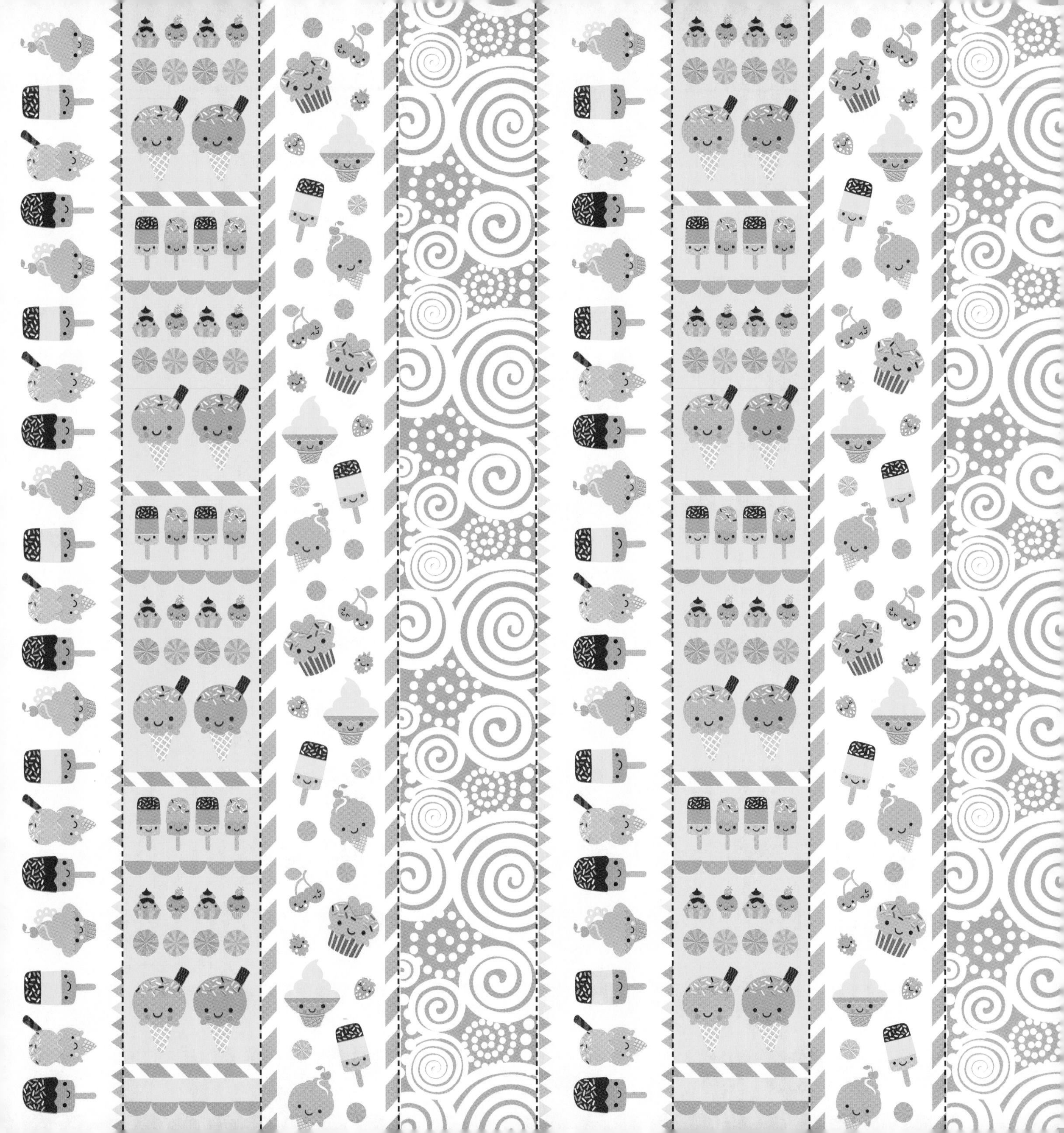

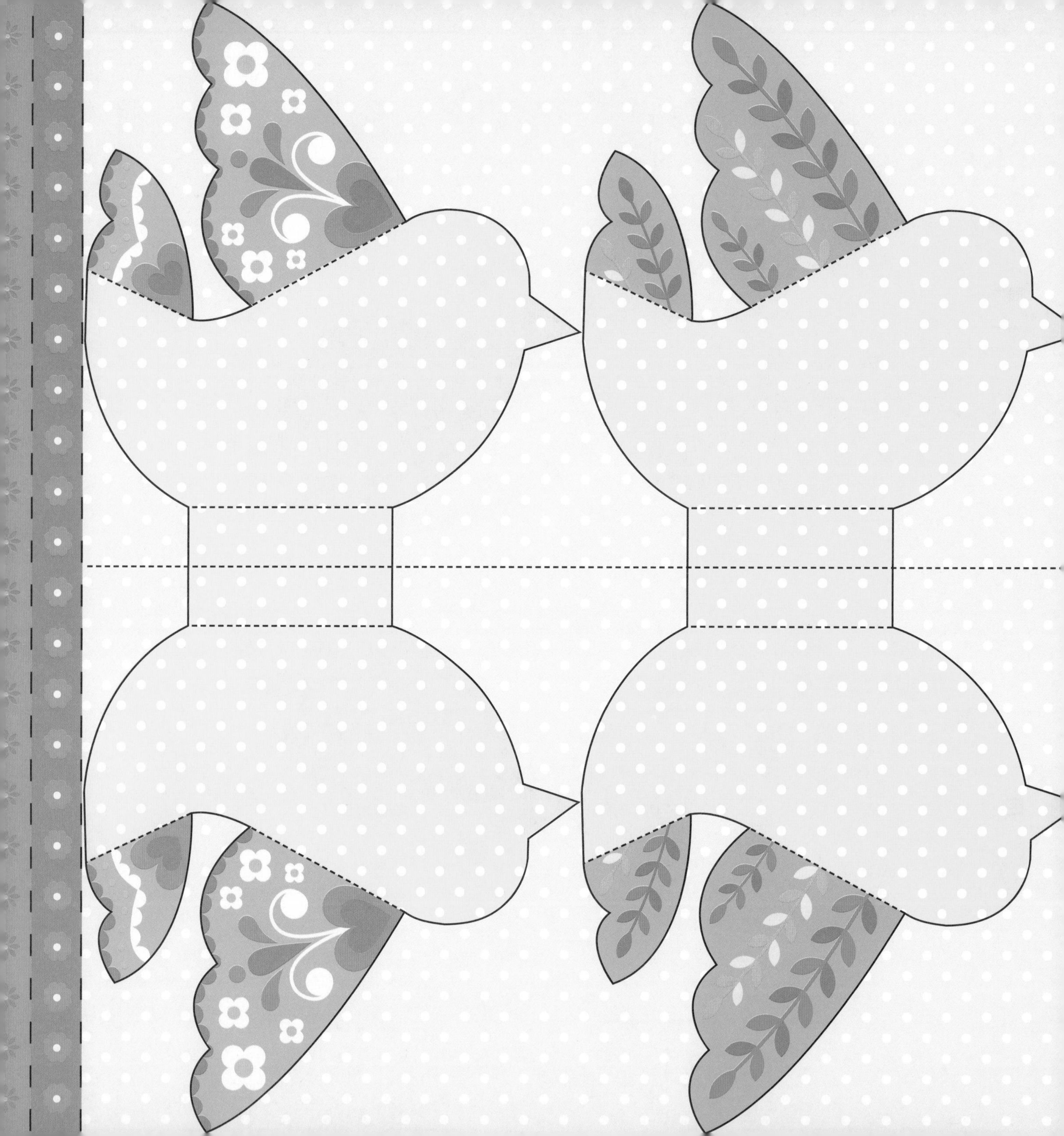

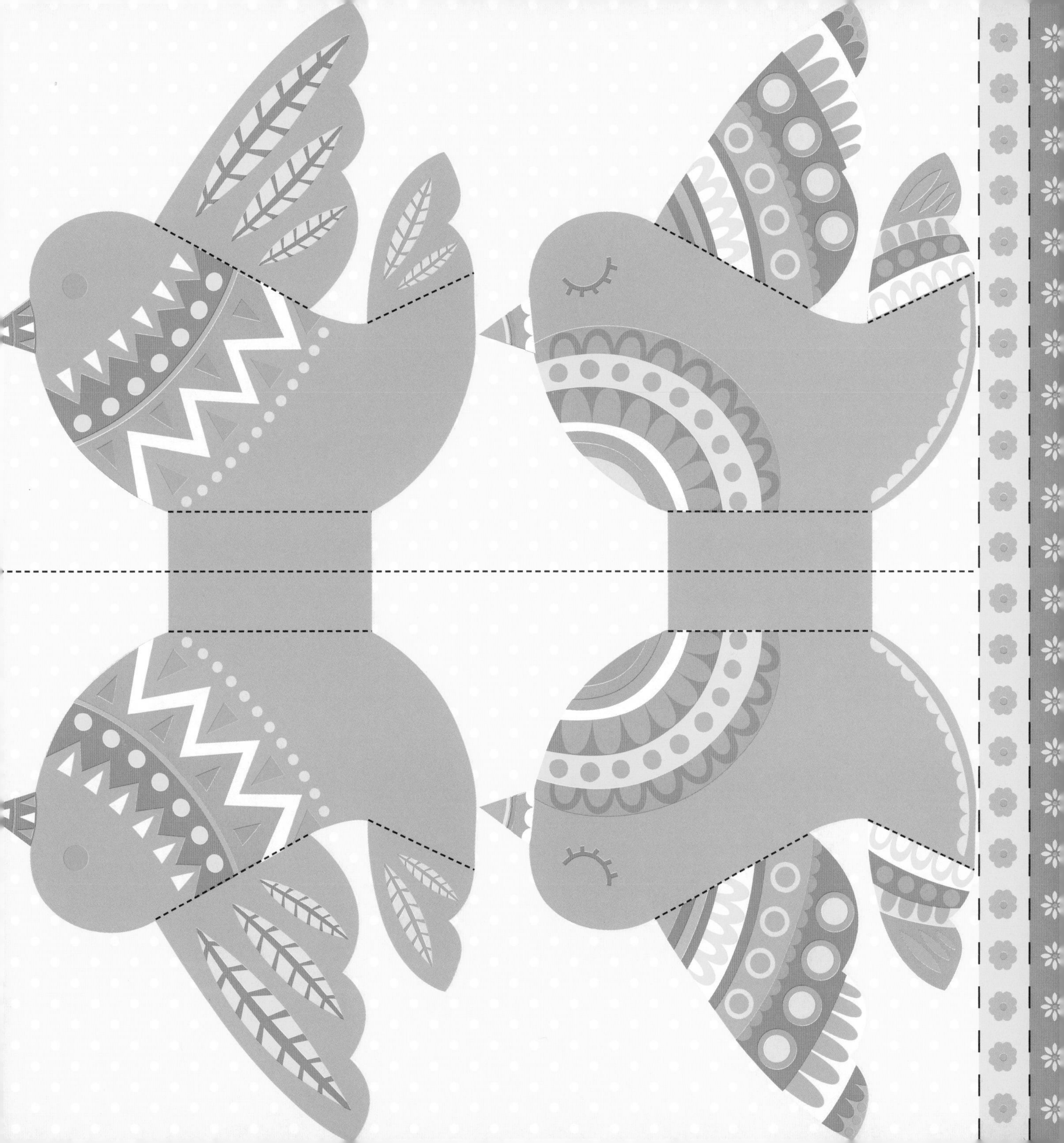

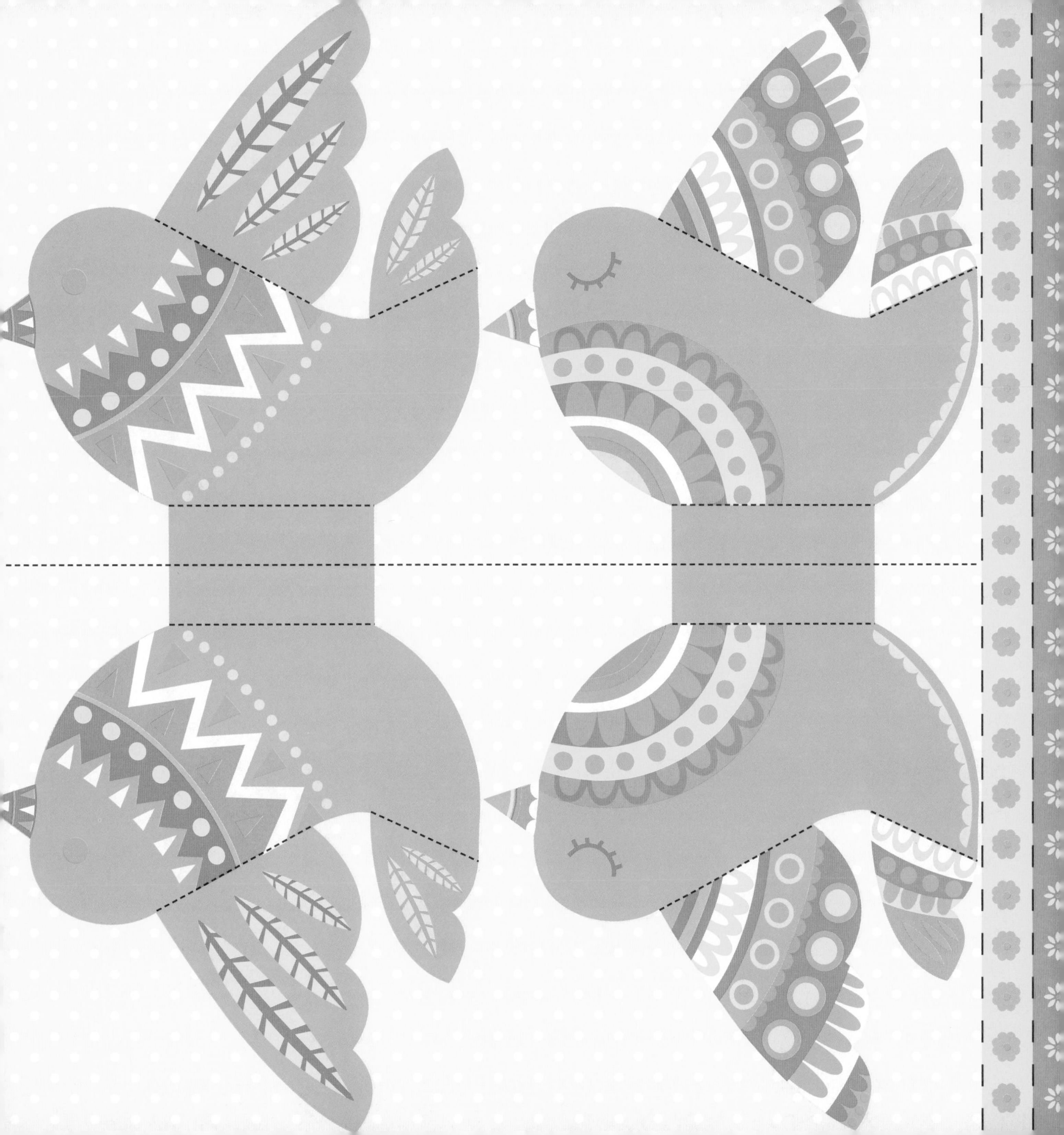

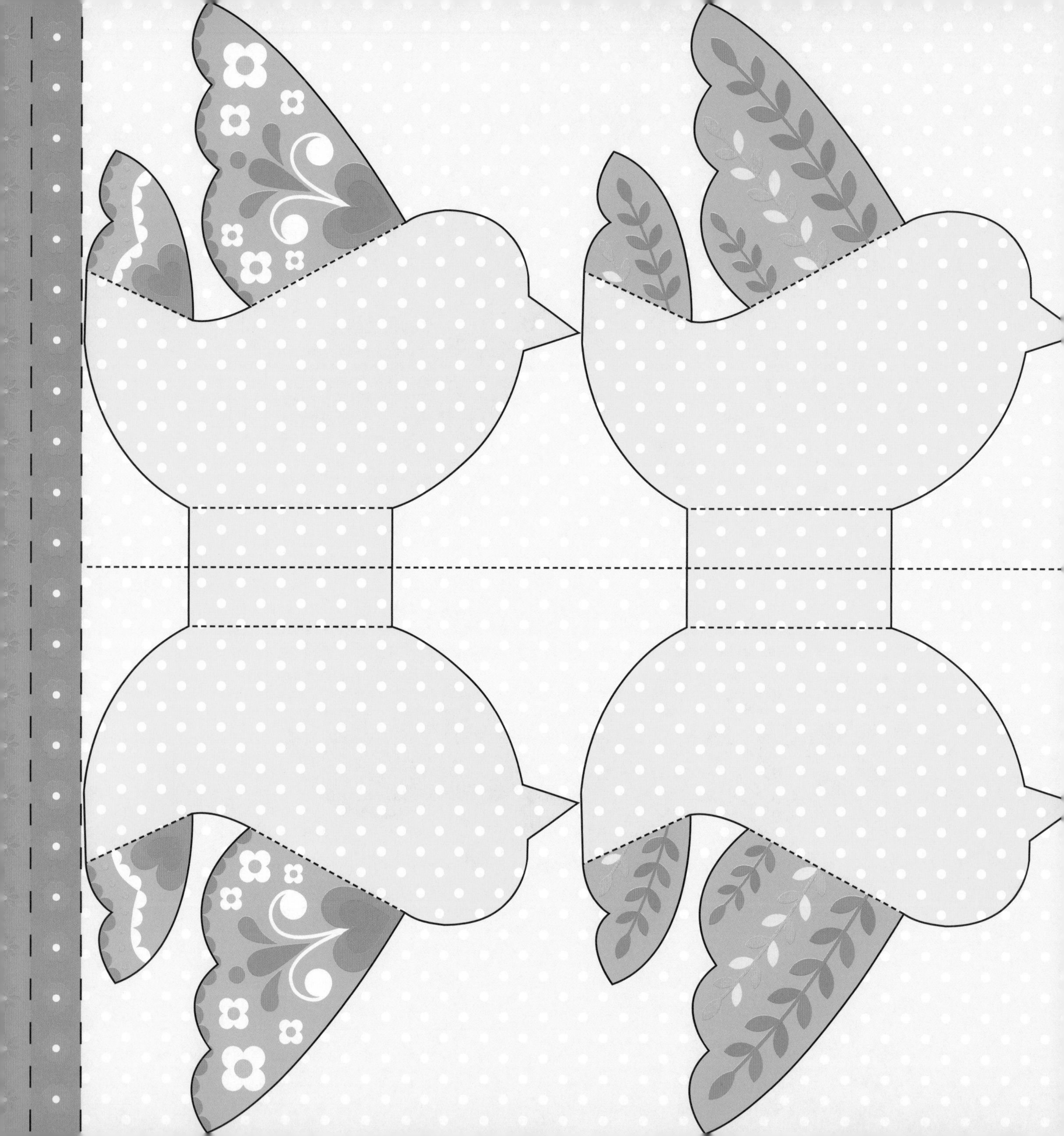

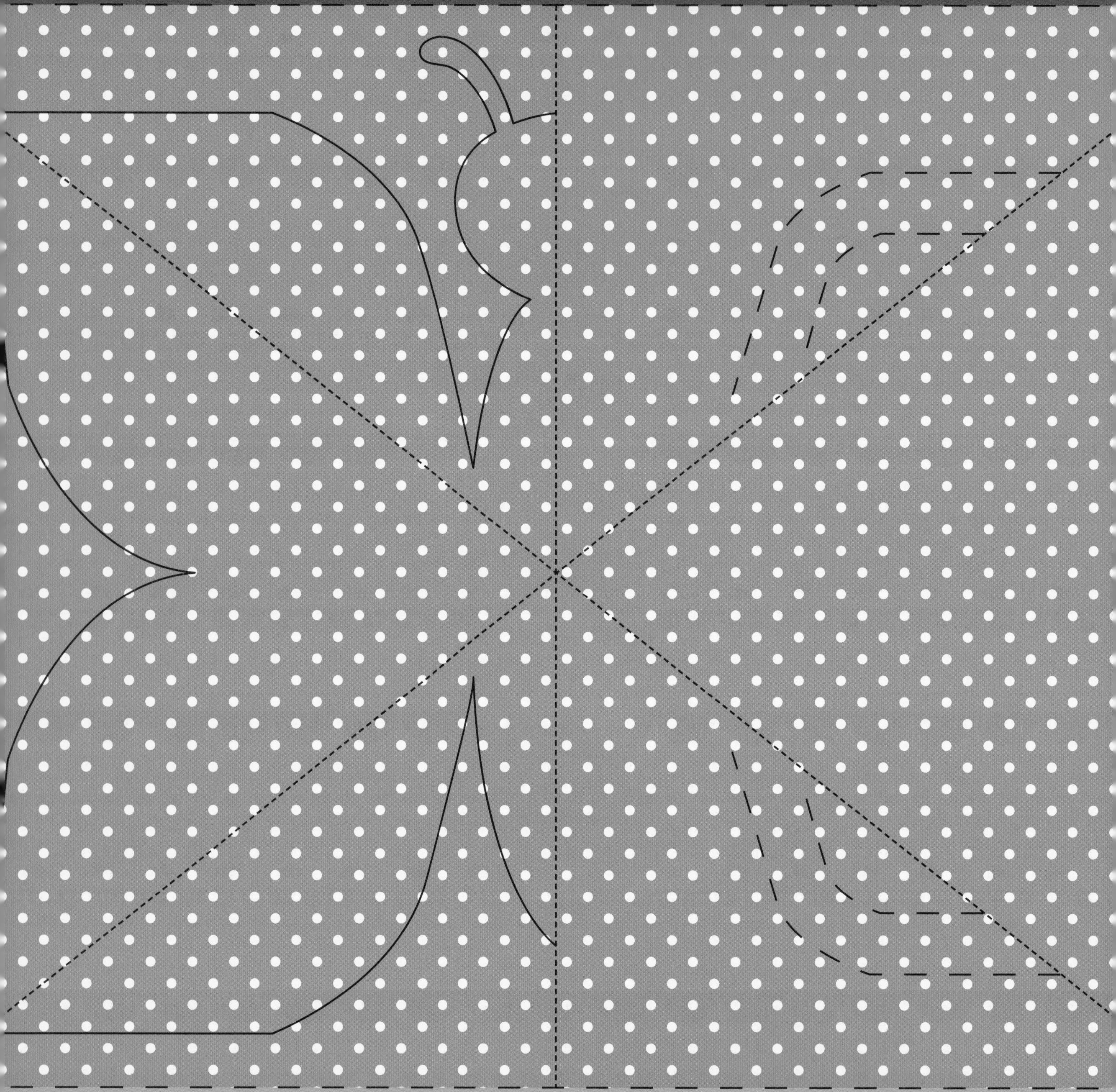